# TEAM ROPING 101

## The Complete Sport from Header to Heeler
### On the Ground, On Your Horse, On Target

KAYLA STARNES

Foreword by Clinton Anderson

TRAFALGAR SQUARE
North Pomfret, Vermont

First published in 2011 by
Trafalgar Square Books
North Pomfret, Vermont 05053

**Printed in China**

**Library of Congress Cataloging-in-Publication Data**
Starnes, Kayla.
   Team roping 101 : the complete sport from header to heeler-- on the ground, on your horse, and on target / Kayla Starnes.
       p. cm.
   Includes index.
     Summary: "A general description of the fast-growing equestrian sport called team roping, with specific instructions for getting started, training your mount, and competing"-- Provided by publisher.
   ISBN 978-1-57076-471-4 (pbk.)
   1.  Team roping.  I. Title. II. Title: Team roping one hundred one. III. Title: Team roping one hundred and one.
   GV1834.45.T42S73 2011
   791.84--dc22
                                                          2011011848
All photos by Kayla Starnes except p. x (Elizabeth Starnes) and figs. 1.2 A-D on p. 17 (courtesy Lone Wolf Photography)
Book design by Carrie Fradkin
Cover design by RM Didier
Typefaces: John Handy, Stones Sans, Stone Informal

10 9 8 7 6 5 4 3 2 1

# Contents

# BUILDING A FOUNDATION 81

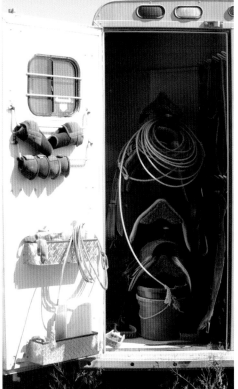

# Foreword

## BY CLINTON ANDERSON

TEAM ROPING is an exhilarating sport that's becoming vastly popular with today's riders. A fast-paced event where split-second decisions make or break a run, team roping is as challenging as it is invigorating, and like everything to do with horses, your success in the sport will depend on your dedication and willingness to educate yourself.

The USTRC and Equibrand®, trusted names in the roping industry, have teamed up to bring you a book with all the information you need to make your venture into the sport successful and long lasting. This book will walk you step by step through picking out the perfect horse to preparing for your first competition, and all the training in between.

As a clinician and the founder of Downunder Horsemanship®, I make my living giving people the tools and knowledge necessary to accomplish their horsemanship dreams—and to stay safe in the process. At every tour stop and clinic I teach, I often see frustrated owners in dangerous situations, not at all enjoying their horses because they chose the wrong horse, are getting pushed around by an 1,100-pound animal, and don't understand how to communicate or cue their horses correctly. So I'm pleased to say that more than just an introduction to team roping, *Team Roping 101* addresses the importance of horsemanship and establishing a partnership with your horse.

In fact, several chapters are dedicated to learning to effectively communicate with your horse and some address common problems that are likely to crop up as you move from the ranks of beginner to experienced competitor. You'll even hear from me several times, explaining the importance of earning your horse's respect, why being able to control your horse's body from his nose to his tail is vital to a good run, and my proven fixes to common problems.

With keen insight from top competitors, trainers, and all-around great horsemen, this book offers a solid first step into the world of team roping. When it comes to horses, learning is constant, and no matter how much you know, there is always more we can all learn. Good luck on your new journey, mate!

**Clinton Anderson**
Downunder Horsemanship
www.downunderhorsemanship.com

# Author's Note

Team roping has historically been a male-dominated activity, but today's enthusiasts are increasingly girls and women who have discovered the thrill of this fast-growing sport. Therefore, I feel it necessary to mention that the choice to refer to all team ropers within this book as "he" (except when in reference to a specific female roper) is simply for the sake of clarity and consistency. It should not be considered a failure to recognize the expanding diversity in this exciting equestrian discipline.

Kayla Starnes

# Acknowledgments

'd first like to recognize the considerable kindness and help of each of the staffs at the United States Team Roping Championships and Trafalgar Square Books. This book would not exist without either of them.

Also, to those who shared their insights for the benefit of novice team ropers, especially professionals Clinton Anderson, Rickey Green, and Speed Williams.

And, to my good-humored models, such as those at the Cowboy Church of Erath County, who roped on some scorching hot summer days.

Last but certainly not least, I'd like to thank my family for their unfailing support.

# About the Author

**T**EAM ROPING 101 author and photographer Kayla Starnes, of Morgan Mill, Texas, has spent the last six years documenting and promoting the equine industry in various capacities, including as a public relations and marketing specialist and media relations liaison for the second-largest breed association in the world; as a freelance writer and photographer for magazines and trade publications; and as a project coordinator and writer for a leading performance products manufacturing conglomerate.

Starnes' writing and photography has been in print across five continents. See some recent photography samples at www.kstarnesphotography.com.

# Welcome to Team Roping

PART **ONE**

# SPEAKING LIKE A ROPER

THE TEAM ROPING COMMUNITY has come to be a unique and distinct culture. Over time, members of this society have invented their own language to describe their sport. If a visit to a local competition leaves you confused, don't worry. Check out some of the key terms I've included here and consider it your "cheat sheet" for your next trip to the arena. While there's no need to read this "mini glossary" in its entirety—or at all—before jumping into the rest of the book, it will help those of you who are new to the sport.

**Added money:** Money added to the purse that was not derived from entry fees.

**Affiliate event:** Refers to United States Team Roping Championships (USTRC) approved ropings around the country. Although they are not sanctioned by the association, USTRC members can compete and acquire applied earnings that count toward earning entry into the Regional and National Final's Shoot-Out divisions.

**Anticipate:** When a horse predicts what will happen next and excitedly responds too soon, it is called *anticipating*. This is a negative thing because the rider wants the horse to wait for the rider's signal.

**Applied earnings (personal earnings):** Earnings acquired as a result of competing at approved USTRC-sanctioned and/or affiliate events.

**Barrier distance:** See *Barrier line (barrier).*

**Barrier line (barrier):** There are, in essence, three *barrier lines* affecting the start of a team roping run; one each for the header, the heeler, and the steer. All are in place to allow the steer a fair head start.  The steer's barrier (also referred to as a "score line") is a line placed in front of the steer's path (usually 10 to 15 feet beyond the chute) that he must reach before the header's horse's nose can pass the header barrier line or the heeler's horse's nose passes the heeler barrier line. The header barrier runs across the front of the header box. The heeler barrier runs across the front of the heeler box. The clock starts when the steer reaches its barrier line. The producer of the roping event, to reflect the arena size and speed of the cattle as well as the designated division of the roping, adjusts the steer's barrier or score line length: The lower the number of the division, the shorter the score line length; the higher the division, the longer the score line length.

**Barrier penalty:** See *Breaking the barrier (breaking out).*

**Bit:** Part of the bridle that goes through the horse's mouth, allowing communication between the rider's hands and the horse's mouth.

**Box:** The three-sided areas behind and on either side of the roping chute facing out toward the arena. Headers on their head horses begin their runs from the heading box to the left of the roping chute, and heelers on their heel horses begin their run in the heeling box to the right of the roping chute. A typical roping box might be 12 feet wide and 16 feet deep.

**Breaking the barrier (breaking out):** When a steer is released from the chute in a team roping run, it is given a 10 to 15 foot head-start. If either rider leaves the box before this distance is reached by the steer, it results in a 5 second penalty and is called "breaking the barrier."

**Bridle catch:** An illegal head catch where the rope hangs in the steer's mouth.

**Burner:** The leather or rawhide patch that is sewn on the end of the eye (hondo). A burner prevents the rope from wearing through the eye and makes the rope slide faster, because drag is reduced. A burner should last the lifetime of the rope.

**Cap:** Refers to the maximum handicap classification number that a roper can have in a particular roping. Example: If a roping is capped at a #5, no roper with a handicap greater than #5 is eligible to compete in the roping.

**Catching:** The act of a roper securing a steer with his rope—either heading or heeling.

**Cheeks:** Between the horse's ears and mouth run the adjustable parts of the bridle headstall that are appropriately called the *cheeks*. One or both cheeks have buckles to tailor length to an individual horse's head.

**Chin strap (curb strap):** Part of the bridle that attaches from one side of the bit to the other and lies in the groove behind the horse's chin.

**Classification:** The numerical rating assigned to an individual USTRC member that ranks his competitive skills. Numbers range from 1 to 10; a #1 is a true beginning roper and a #10 is a professional.

**Coils:** Excess rope between the *loop* and the *tail* is gathered neatly into the hand not swinging the loop by rolling into these manageable circles.

**Concave:** Curved or rounded inward.

**Concho:** An exterior metal part of a Western saddle; usually decorative as well as functional. There are generally four (two per side) on a saddle.

**Corner:** In a team roping run, after the header has secured (caught) the steer and dallied, the rules require that the team turn the steer to the left. The point at which the steer turns left is referred to as the "corner." It is also the point at which the heeler must turn in order to attempt his catch.

**Correction bit:** A type of shanked bit (leverage bit) with a stiff port.

**Corriente:** Breed of cattle originating in Mexico especially suited for team roping. Cattle are both imported and bred for the sport in the United States.

**Counterbending:** One of horse trainer Clinton Anderson's exercises to gain greater control of a horse. In it, the horse's nose is tipped *away* from the direction the horse's shoulders are going. Counterbending should be practiced in both directions and eventually, at all three gaits.

**Dally (dallying):** The act of wrapping the rope around the saddle horn in order to secure the steer after it's been roped. A dally is considered to be one full wrap of the rope around the saddle horn.

**Dally rubber:** Used on the saddle horn, this is a circle of flexible material that resembles an oversized rubber band. It serves a couple of purposes. First, it prevents rope from slipping on the horn when a roper dallies. Second, it protects the horn from rope burns should the rope slip.

**Double numbers:** A roper may have different classifications for heading and heeling. When this is the case, they have two numerical ratings, hence "double numbers."

**Dragger:** A steer that drags its hind legs and will not hop. This kind of steer is difficult for a heeler to catch.

**Dry spots:** When a saddle is removed from the horse after a ride, sometimes dry areas appear on an otherwise damp, sweaty back. These can be caused by an improperly fitting saddle and should be investigated.

**Eliminator:** Steer that is nearly impossible to rope and eliminates a roper from the average of a roping.

**Eye (hondo):** Where one end of the rope forms a small ring that the rest of the rope threads through to form a loop.

**Facing:** At the conclusion of a team roping run, after the heeler has caught the steer, the header must turn (face) his horse toward the steer. When both partners have secured the steer and their horses are facing the steer with ropes dallied and tight, the run is over and time is taken.

**Flex Earnings:** Earnings that are allocated as a direct result of winning a Regional or National Shoot-Out position at an approved, USTRC-sanctioned event. Flex Earnings can be used at a roper's discretion at either the Regional

Finals or the National Finals, and with a partner of choice. Flex Earnings do not carry over from season to season and therefore expire at the end of each season.

- USTRC will allocate $6,000 for a National Shoot-Out—$3,000 per partner
- USTRC will allocate $2,000 for a Regional Shoot-Out—$1,000 per partner

**Floor:** Refers to the minimum classification number a roper must have in order to participate in a specific roping. For example, if a competition has a "#6 floor," no roper with a classification less than a #6 is eligible to enter.

**Four-headers:** A roping competition of four rounds over which teams progressively rope four steers. The team with the fastest aggregate time on its four steers wins the roping.

**Full:** Refers to rope diameter. It means the diameter is slightly larger than a standard measurement.

**Full go-rounds:** A full go-round is a round where every roper entered is given the opportunity to rope (see *Progressive after*).

**Ground money:** A term that originally meant competitors received their entry fees back as a prize consideration. In recent years, it has been interpreted to mean multiples of the entry fee.

**Hazing:** The act of guiding a steer in a particular direction while on horseback. During the course of a team roping run the heeler *hazes* the steer or keeps the steer moving straight to slightly left down the arena. This allows his partner/header to gain quicker position on the steer in order to make the catch.

**Head catch:** There are three legal head catches in the sport of team roping: (1) around both horns; (2) around half a head (the neck and one horn); or (3) around the neck.

**Head-ducking:** Sometimes, experienced cattle learn habits to attempt to evade capture, like lowering their head when a header's loop is thrown. This makes them harder to catch.

**Head horse:** The horse that is ridden by the header or a horse that is usually used for heading.

**Header:** The roper who catches the head, horns, or neck of the steer.

**Headstall:** The part of the horse's bridle that holds everything in place on the horse's head.

**Heat (rotation):** A set number of ropers that rope all rounds prior to the short round, before the next *heat* has the opportunity to compete.

**Heel catch:** A catch where the loop encircles the steer's hind legs anywhere from above the hooves to the top of the hip. Catching only one heel is a legal catch but results in a 5-second penalty.

**Heel horse:** The horse that is ridden by the heeler or a horse that is usually used for heeling.

**Heeler:** The roper who catches the steer's hind legs.

**Hondo:** See *Eye*.

**Incentive:** As it relates to team roping, an incentive is a roping within a roping. A separate pool of money is set aside from the regular payout pool. This cash can only be won by those ropers who meet the stated incentive criteria of a roping. A typical *Incentive* would be where a #10 roping is stated to have a #9 Incentive. In this case, a portion of the fees from all the #9 teams entered is set aside, and can only be won by those teams that are classified as #9 or less. Those teams are also eligible to win money in the overall payout.

**Keeper:** Small loop of leather, or similar material, on the horse's breast collar that holds a tie-down strap close to the breast collar. This prevents the horse's leg from tangling in the tie-down.

**Kick:** Describes a process in the manufacturing of a rope. The amount of *kick* applied to the loop makes it easier or harder to swing.

**Lap-and-tap start:** Roping without a barrier. This method pre-dates the use of chutes.

**Lateral flexion:** The act of taking up one rein to direct the horse's nose toward the stirrup on the same side.

**Lay (stiffness):** Determined by how tightly twisted the strands of the rope are wound. There are seven different lay choices: Double extra-soft; extra-soft; soft; medium-soft; medium; medium-hard; and hard. Softer lays are typically used for heading, where most ropers use an extra-soft or soft lay. Firmer lays are primarily used by heelers, where medium-soft to medium-hard lays are the most popular choice.

**Limited entry:** Refers to enter one time and enter twice events, as opposed to the more traditional multiple entry competitions, where ropers have numerous partners.

**Loop:** When the tail of the rope is passed through the eye, a circle of rope is formed. Properly sized, this is what the roper actually swings around his head and throws to catch a steer. Correct loop size is different for each roper; however, beginners should have larger loops than more experienced ropers. As a general rule, a loop's diameter should be the distance from a hand outstretched at shoulder height to the ground.

**Mohair blend:** Made from natural mohair fibers, blended with a significant portion of non-mohair fibers.

**Muley:** A genetically hornless, or polled, steer. May be used in place of horned stock, especially in geographic areas where those breeds are scarce.

**Multiple entry events:** Competition format that allows a roper to participate with multiple partners in a given division.

**National Finals of Team Roping (National Finals):** The premier championship event of the USTRC. Ropers must qualify for the competition, which is held annually in Oklahoma City, Oklahoma.

**Natural mohair:** Made from mohair fibers, usually 100 percent.

**Non-sanctioned events:** Events not sanctioned by the USTRC. They do not qualify a competitor to a USTRC Regional or Cinch National Finals event.

**Non-shanked:** A non-leverage bit.

**No-time:** When either roper misses catching the steer in competition, their score (time) is not recorded.

**Partnerability:** One of the 10 performance markers USTRC factors into establishing a roper's classification (see p. 22). This marker evaluates the quality of the ropers an individual has roped with and how popular or desirable he is to other ropers as a partner.

**Peer votes:** Produced by fellow ropers—who are invited to vote on individual ratings through a ballot at varying times throughout a given season—to help classify other ropers (see *Screenings*).

**Pigtail:** The short part of a rope barrier that breaks away when the barrier is broken.

**Point of purchase:** On the mouthpiece of the horse's bit where the shank connects.

**Progressive after:** This term means that when you miss, you are eliminated. For example, *progressive after one* means that from the very beginning of the roping, after you miss one steer, you are eliminated. It is not always a single head that determines this. For example, if an event is *progressive after two*, a roper is guaranteed two steers. However, anything missed beyond those two runs is "sudden death."

**Pull barrier:** A rope barrier that must be "pulled" or stretched across the opening of the box.

**Rate:** The ability of a horse to adjust his speed relative to the speed of the steer (see *Tracking*).

**Regional Finals:** smaller-scaled versions of the pinnacle competition of the sport—the National Finals of Team Roping. These regional championship events were created when the USTRC realized many qualified ropers wanted to attend a premium roping closer to their home and at a more affordable cost than the National Finals.

**Reins:** Part of the bridle between the bit and the rider's hand(s). Roping reins are a single looped strap.

**Rope:** Arguably the most important piece of gear in team roping, this is what the header and heeler use to catch the steer. (Learn more about ropes, including parts and selection, in chapter 2, p. 31.)

**Rope bag:** A specially-designed bag meant to carry and protect a roper's common gear, including ropes.

**Rotation:** See *Heat*.

**Sanctioned events (qualifier):** USTRC-recognized and approved events that meet specific standards stipulated by the USTRC, such as: formats of the ropings, quality of the production, and prize requirements, among others. These ropings are open to all USTRC members and qualify entrants for a Regional or National Finals championship event.

**Scant:** Refers to rope diameter. This term means the diameter is slightly smaller than a standard measurement.

**Screenings**: Obtained from trained staff who are sent to select events to evaluate ropers' ability. Ranked by order of importance to a competition, *screenings* allow members to be classified appropriately and objectively (see *Peer votes*).

**Shank:** A piece of metal that drops from the mouthpiece of a bit to where the rein attaches, creating leverage that can be used as a means to control the horse.

**Short round:** The final or last round of a roping.

**Score line length:** How much of a head start the steer is given before the ropers are allowed to the leave the box. Average distance is 10 to 15 feet, depending on arena size.

**Scoring (score):** The ability of a rider to control his horse at the beginning of a team roping run so that the horse begins chasing the steer *only* upon the rider's command. The intention is to have the horse reach the head or heel barrier a fraction of a second after the steer has tripped the score length barrier.

**Spoke:** The area of the loop between the eye and the hand that grasps the loop. The *spoke* consists of two strands of rope—top and bottom.

**Steer:** Male castrated bovine animal.

**Synthetic neoprene:** Manufactured product used to create cinches and other tack. It is anti-microbial and anti-fungal, which is beneficial in a hot, humid climate.

**Tail:** The opposite of the eye, this is the other end of the rope that terminates in a knot.

**TBA:** The abbreviation for the term "To Be Announced"—many ropers who do not have partners before the draw have the option to pay for both sides and put "TBA" in the vacant position.

**Tie-down keeper:** See *Keeper.*

**Tie on:** Refers to practice of tying the heeling rope to the saddle horn, versus dallying. Women of any age and men 55 years of age and older are allowed this option. Children under the age of 12 are forbidden from tying on. For complete regulations about this subject, refer to the *USTRC Rulebook.*

**Tip:** When the loop is swung, the *tip* is the point farthest from the roper. Centrifugal force gives a tip weight, similar to a person swinging a bucket of water: The same way the water doesn't slosh from the bucket because the force keeps it in, the tip also pushes out with weight away from the roper during the swing.

**Tracking:** The act of following a steer from horseback. The horse is expected to maintain a proper position relative to the steer's pattern and speed (see *Rate*).

**Tug:** The part of the horse's breast collar that runs from the center of the chest, between the front legs, and snaps on to the front cinch.

**Turnout:** Refers to a steer being released from the chute at the request of a judge when a team is not present to compete.

**Up and back:** This is the practice of two ropers entering with "Roper A" heading and "Roper B" heeling, then entering again in the same roping with "Roper B" heading and "Roper A" heeling.

**United States Team Roping Championships (USTRC):** The primary governing body of the sport of team roping. Its jurisdiction extends beyond the United States.

**Vertical flexion:** When a horse drops his head and tucks his nose, *flexing* at the poll.

**Wool felt:** A non-woven fabric, formed when wool is subjected to heat, moisture, and pressure or agitation.

INTRODUCTION TO AMERICA'S
# COWBOY SPORT

"FRANKLY, A GUY without a rope is just a boy and his horse."

"World's Greatest Horseman" Russell Dilday spoke these words moments after receiving this prestigious title from the National Reined Cow Horse Association in 2008. The competition he won to earn it was made up of a marathon of different Western events, and it speaks volumes that he mentioned roping when summing up his achievement.

Roping—especially *team* roping—has played an important and growing part in defining modern horsemen and horsewomen in recent years. Whether you enjoy the adrenaline rush of high-speed action, want the chance to win big cash payouts and glittering championship buckles, or seek the opportunity to build lifelong friendships, team roping is a competition tailored to you. It's a sport for everyone, from age 8 to 80, with skill levels from the beginner to the professional.

## WHAT IS TEAM ROPING?

The team roping event that takes place today is virtually unchanged from the early range days when cowboys doctored and branded cattle. At its most basic level, team roping is a speed sport that consists of a pair of riders attempting to quickly catch a loose steer with two ropes around the steer's horns and heels.

Teamwork is the key to success in this event; teamwork between two ropers and teamwork between each roper and his horse. Team roping may be held as a stand-alone competition or as one of six recognized events during a rodeo. Stand-alone events—which are this book's focus—can have more than one division, which are broken into levels for all ropers, from beginners to pros. Ropers can compete in multiple divisions with different partners, which can make for a great day or weekend of competition.

Stand-alone events may require multiple *rounds*, or *runs*, to determine the winning team. This determination is made based on the team's cumulative average of each round's time.

This multiple-round format gives a roper more than one chance to earn a score. Usually, individuals have four separate runs, known as *four-steer averages* or *four-headers*, which means that the winning team must catch four steers consecutively and make its runs cumulatively faster than any other team in the event. If a team misses even a single steer, it is out of the running. This is called *progressive*

1.1 A–D  *Here, a pair of teens—Paul Melvin and Whitney Green—practice the timed event. Paul catches the steer by the horns, dallies, and prepares to turn left into the corner, while Whitney "hazes" the steer, or encourages it to run straight by running alongside (A). After Paul turns the steer left, Whitney repositions her horse to just off the steer's left hip (B). Once she is in place, Whitney makes her throw to catch the steer's two hind feet in her loop (C). When she catches, she pulls the rope tight and dallies it around her horn, signaling her horse to stop, and Paul pivots his horse around and backs him up to help take up any remaining slack in the rope (D). As soon as both riders' ropes are taut, the run is finished.*

*after*, another term for "sudden death," which means when you miss, you are eliminated from competition. However, while the overall fastest time wins, often winners of the quickest individual time are also awarded prizes and cash.

What do the stages of a successful team roping run look like (figs. 1.1 A–D and 1.2 A–D)? Mimicking skills born on the range, each individual run begins with a steer in a chute and ropers on horseback to each side. A typical roping arena is 300 feet by 150 feet. The chute is located just off-center to the right, at one end of the arena. It is flanked on each side by the box. The box is where the two horseback ropers—the team—start.

The run begins with a nod from the roper on the left, the *header*, to the person in charge of releasing the steer. This nod signals that the team is ready. Then, the steer is released and given a 10- to 15-foot head start—known as *the score*. Until the steer crosses its allowed head start, the ropers should wait to cross their designated *barrier (barrier line)*. These barriers stretch across the front of each box and are marked by a rope or an electronic beam.

The steer usually runs straight down the center of the arena toward the opposite end, where an open exit gate leads him back to his herdmates. However, the goal of the two team ropers is to stop the steer's dash by roping it.

So, after the barrier distance is achieved, the riders sprint to catch up to the steer, each staying on his respective side. The header, who breaks from the left of the chute, is the first to try to catch, aiming for the horns or neck. Once done, he secures his loop by wrapping the extra length of rope rapidly around his saddle horn, which is called *dallying*. After dallying, the header guides his horse into a left-hand turn, known as the *corner*, pulling the steer behind. This positions it for the other teammate, the *heeler*, to make his catch.

The heeler has an important function right out of the box. First, he must *haze* the steer, which simply means maintaining a specific position off to the right side of the steer. This position encourages the steer to keep running in a straight line and allows the header the best chance at catching it.

After the header catches, and turns the steer into the corner, the heeler follows the steer into the turn to make his catch, encircling both of the steer's hind feet with the rope. It is key for the heeler to gauge the rhythm of the steer's gait in order to precisely place the loop for the steer to step through. The heeler finishes by dallying, while simultaneously stopping his horse. At that point, the header turns his horse around toward the steer, called *facing*. He maintains a taut rope by backing his horse up when needed, but the steer does not need to be pulled off its feet to the ground for the run to qualify.

A judge, who is also known as a *flagman* or *flagger*, is in the arena and calls the run. The official, who is on horseback, waits until both ropes are taut and each roper's horse is facing the steer. At that moment, the flagger drops the flag in his raised hand, signaling the timekeeper to stop the clock and record the team's time, which can typically range from 5 to 15 seconds.

**1.2 A–D** *Beginning with a bird's eye view of the start of a team roping run, here's a series from a competition. In photo A, the steer leaves the chute (center), while the team ropers leave the box, which is the blue pipe structure that surrounds the chute. The box serves as a starting gate for both riders. The header's horse (left) is just pushing past the barrier with its chest. Horseback onlookers at the bottom of the photo are other ropers, waiting their turn. As in Whitney and Paul's practice run, the header catches the steer by the horns, then turns it left as the heeler gets into position (B & C). At a competition, the flagger or flagman (background) waits to call the run (D). This official judge ends the run and stops the timer by lowering the flag held in his hand. He rides nearby in order to see clearly any penalties a team may incur or to help should there be an emergency. (Photos Courtesy Lone Wolf Photography)*

*Introduction to America's Cowboy Sport*

Penalties can be added to a team's total elapsed time for rule infractions, such as *breaking the barrier* or *breaking-out*, which is when a team begins chasing the steer before it has traveled its allotted head start. This penalty adds 10 extra seconds to the time. Another common penalty is if the heeler is only able to rope a single hind foot, which is worth 5 added seconds. Of course, if either teammate misses their target completely, which lets the steer escape; they receive no score for their run at all, also called a *no-time*.

## A SPORT OF NATIONAL REPRESENTATION

The modern sport of team roping is primarily governed by the United States Team Roping Championships (USTRC) and is a fairly straightforward athletic event to understand. The USTRC is a membership organization, which was formed in 1990 with two major goals in mind.

The first was to create a national classification rating or handicap system that ranks ropers on their individual ability. Its purpose was to open the sport to all ages and skill levels of ropers, from novice to professional. Prior to this time, most team ropings were of a "jackpot" variety—that is, open to all comers, regardless of skill. Unless you were very good, your chances of earning prize money were slim.

By assessing the roping level of both partners, and then combining this information into a team handicap, today's roping divisions are formed by segmenting the handicapped teams along a graduated scale of ability. The USTRC wasn't the first to invent a handicap system, but in just a few short years, its version has become the de facto classification framework for the entire United States.

The second original goal of the USTRC was to create a national championship event where team ropers could come together in one arena, at all skill levels, and compete for the title of United States Champion. That goal has been achieved with the Cinch National Finals of Team Roping (NFTR). The Cinch National Finals is the USTRC's annual year-end event, usually held in the fall. Since its inception, this premier competition has become the largest and richest recreational team roping event in the world. In a single year, it has had as many as 8,000 different teams entered and awarded more than $5.5 million dollars in cash and prizes during its nine-day run.

## HOME ON THE RANGE

Like all Western disciplined equine activities, team roping has its roots in the American ranching culture (fig. 1.3). The act of two horsemen roping a steer has always been regarded as a safe, humane method to handle large cattle and

1.3 *Team roping has its roots in American ranching culture, which involves the care and maintenance of land and livestock, and even today often requires many hours in the saddle.*

is still an effective technique used in modern cattle-ranching operations. The technique takes away two of a cow's main defenses—horns and heels—making it safer for people on foot to approach to administer medicine or to inspect for signs of illness or parasites.

On the range, the mission is just to catch and hold the cattle. In the arena, it's to do it fast and with style.

The sport of rodeo stems from these and other skills required in the practice of working cattle. Roping has long been included in rodeo's line up of events, although only in the past few decades has team roping evolved to the form we recognize today.

Modern team roping made its debut at the Professional Rodeo Cowboys Association (PRCA) National Finals Rodeo (NFR) in the 1970s, when it began as an offshoot of the single horse-and-rider, tie-down calf roping event. Since that time, the sport has progressed rapidly and with it, competitor skill level.

## NATIONALIZING TEAM ROPING

Before the USTRC's formation in 1990, several regional organizations existed to govern modern recreational team roping. However, there was no national governing body for the sport. Unethical ropers could cheat the various classification systems by simply changing the association in which they competed.

Founder Denny Gentry began the USTRC with the purpose of developing an organization that would become a nationwide authority for the United States, standardizing classifications and providing a fair, level playing field for ropers in all areas of the country.

Gentry also set out to track ropers with a computer database. The database idea was a novel concept at that time, when only a minority of the membership was familiar with or comfortable using computers. Over the years, the database system has proven to be a successful model. It has stood the test of time for more than two decades and has provided the sport with the ability to study patterns for entry and competitive purposes. Most telling is the fact that roping producers who are not affiliated with the organization still rely on its classification system to ensure fair competition.

## A MODERN PASTIME

Team roping has progressed in the last few years to reach the sophistication of many modern athletic events, and its popularity has grown exponentially over the past couple of decades.

In fact, according to the USTRC, team roping is one of America's largest and fastest growing equine sports. The organization tracked approximately 12,000 competitors when it launched the first computerized database in 1990. Since then, the USTRC has classified more than 150,000 individuals and still continues to track many of them today at the more than 400 sanctioned and affiliate roping competitions held each year. With over 35,000 members at the time of writing, the USTRC adds an average of 70 new members every week.

Today, the USTRC is highly regarded for its production standards. The organization has always prided itself on the air of formality and punctuality that sets its competitions apart. Another point of pride is its cash award distribution format, which allows it to offer the richest prize package of any team roping group and—with the possible exception of cutting—any other equine sport.

The USTRC awarded more than $20 million in prize money to ropers at sanctioned events during 2010. Its premier competition—the National Finals of Team Roping—has awarded more than $3 million dollars in cash each year since 2002. During 2010, ropers took home more than $4.2 million in cash and prizes from that event.

# THE DIFFERENCE BETWEEN RODEO AND USTRC EVENTS

Today, USTRC-governed team roping competition has moved far from its rodeo roots, although ropers do often participate in both arenas. The two are similar in that they both are pay-to-play sports. That is, competitors pay an entry fee and the winnings that are distributed come from these fees plus, in some cases, added money provided by the event producer.

The two, however, have some important differences. For example, a PRCA rodeo features team roping as just one of several different types of competition. It also includes events like barrel racing, bronc riding, and bull riding. In contrast, USTRC competition specializes in the single discipline. Also, rodeo team ropers only compete in one or two rounds, but USTRC events typically require a team to catch four steers before competition is complete. This format places the emphasis on consistently good times instead of spectacular individual runs.

This changes the strategy used by ropers in each type of team roping competition. Rodeo places more emphasis on blisteringly fast individual runs, because ropers have one shot to get it right. A miss equals elimination there. Although swiftness is still very much a factor at USTRC events, putting consecutive successful runs together is more important than raw speed. As a result, with the exception of elite USTRC competitors, rodeo events tend to have faster times for single runs.

At a USTRC roping, where *average*, or cumulative, times are what matter most; ropers are more conservative when rushing across the barrier. The roper may allow the steer to run a little further down the arena and take a few more swings of the rope to get the best shot at catching it. In the lower skill level divisions, *catching* is the critical aspect—speed isn't as important a factor. Oftentimes, if your team can catch four steers in a row, you will win money.

While USTRC ropings are more about consistency than speed, especially in the amateur ranks, the emphasis gradually changes as you move up to the higher level divisions. Here, not only must a team *catch*, it needs to be fast in doing so. The modern-day USTRC open division events have become so competitive that in a typical competition, "pros" have to make the equivalent of multiple lightning-fast rodeo runs in a row to win. The higher the level of competition, the more it's likely to be about speed as well as consistency.

And, it is getting faster in both arenas. ESPN's sports news-on-line network was one of the first media outlets to report when professional team roping saw a new world record for speed set on December 12, 2009, at the PRCA Wrangler® National Finals in Las Vegas, Nevada. According to ESPN's coverage of the event that night, JoJo Lemond of Andrews, Texas, and Randon Adams of Logandale, Nevada, roped a steer in a blistering 3.4 seconds.

A few minutes later, that record-making time was shattered when Chad Masters, of Clarksville, Tennessee, and Jade Corkill, of Fallon, Nevada, finished their run in only 3.3 seconds.

By the time this book is printed, the world record for a single team roping run may very well have been lowered yet again.

## WELCOME TO TEAM ROPING

Every sport has rules that allow for fair competition, and team roping is no different. Once you have decided to investigate the sport, begin by arming yourself with some understanding of the basics. A great place to start is at the source— the official *USTRC Rulebook*—where readers can find information on everything from becoming a member to competition structure. The USTRC has spent decades fine-tuning these rules, and it is a good idea to review them annually.

Available either online or in print, the *Rulebook* is updated regularly. You can request a printed edition from the USTRC by phone (254.968.0002), or you can download the latest digital version by visiting ustrc.com/Rulebook.

### Classification System

One of the first things a team roper will be asked for—either by event staff or other ropers—is his *classification number*, also known as a *handicap number*. A classification number indicates a roper's skill level or ability and is based on the USTRC's Team Roping Information and Data (TRIAD) classification system. This is true whether you compete yet or not, and all association members are assigned a classification that ranks their ability. So, it's important to know something about this system and why you will be rated a specific number.

The purpose of any good classification system is to maintain an even playing field. A long-standing example is the sport of golf, where the U.S. Golf Association works to maintain a handicap on all golfers. This handicap is based on a record of performance by each golfer under a defined environment. The USTRC's TRIAD system is very much the same.

#### TRIAD System

With the TRIAD system, every header is classified on a scale from #1 through #9 and every heeler 1 through 10, with the numbers 1 through 4 being *novice* classifications, 5 to 7 ranked as *amateur* ropers, and 8 through 10 noted as *professionals*.

The numbers of the header and the heeler are then added to form a team total. For example, a #5 header combined with a 6 heeler would equal a team total of 11, a #8 header with a 5 heeler would equal 13, and so forth.

With a few exceptions, any number header can rope with any number heeler. The team combination total determines the division for which the two ropers qualify. For example, if the team combination total is 13, that team can rope in any division numbered 13 or above, and a team total of 10 allows ropers to compete in any division equal to 10 or higher.

## Divisions

A typical USTRC-sanctioned roping also features eight descending divisions: Open, #15, #13, #12, #11, #10, #9, and the #8 Pick/Draw. In the Open division there is no defined classification handicap, which means the elite professional can compete there. In the smallest-numbered division, the #8 Pick/Draw, ropers don't need to come with a partner in mind. Instead, they can find a partner through a random, computerized draw.

One of the great virtues of this system is that it encourages the more skilled and experienced ropers to rope with the less skilled, inexperienced entrants. Most events employ a concept known as *limited entry*, which means ropers are only allowed to enter a given division a maximum of two to four times. Thus, if a roper wants to enter more often, a likely solution is for him or her to enter in a different, lower division by finding a less skilled roper to compete with. It is for this reason that you often find experienced ropers encouraging and working to help the more green ropers.

## Individual Classifications

To establish each roper's classification, the USTRC's new TRIAD computer database gathers information on 10 common markers in a roper's performance, including speed, consistency, money spent, money won, "partnerability," entry patterns, arena conditions, strength of cattle, length of score, and free form results.

**Speed:** Determined by the amount of time it takes the roper to complete the run. This can be affected by the roper's horsemanship ability and "partnerability," as well as arena conditions, length of score, and strength of cattle.

**Consistency:** Evaluated by the roper's ability to put runs together in succession.

**Money spent:** A record of the events or total amount of money the roper has spent in order to compete.

**Money won:** A record of how much money a roper has won in the number of times he or she has entered an event in each division or in total.

**"Partnerability":** This marker evaluates the quality of the ropers this individual has roped with, and how popular or desirable he is to other ropers as a partner.

**Entry patterns:** An evaluation of the number of times a roper enters a roping competition and in what divisions. This information is especially important relative to the amount of money the roper spent entering that event and the return of money won there.

**Arena conditions:** An evaluation of the conditions under which the roper had to perform, such as indoors or out, and inclement weather conditions, like rain, heat, and freezing cold.

**Strength of cattle:** Determined by how fast the steer leaves the chute and moves down the arena, as well as how much "play" the steer gives the end of the rope after being roped.

**Length of score:** The number of feet the steer is allowed to gain a head start on the roper before the roper is allowed to leave the roping box without a barrier penalty.

**Free form:** These are results reported from rodeos or other competitions for which the USTRC does not have a complete roster. The Association combs through hundreds of results—published in roping publications and provided by producers—in order to classify ropers based on complete data, not just sanctioned events.

Two subjective markers worth mentioning are *screenings* and *peer votes*. Screenings are obtained from trained staff sent to select events to evaluate ropers' ability. These screenings allow members to be classified appropriately and objectively. And, peer votes are produced by fellow ropers, who are invited to vote on individual ratings through a ballot at varying times throughout a given season. (You can learn more about getting classified in chapter 8, p. 126.)

## DEFINING YOUR AMBITIONS

After watching team roping, many spectators set a goal to explore how they would fare in such competition. The challenge of horsemanship combined with precision roping while working with a partner, is an exciting combination for many men and women. It can be a fun weekend pastime, or a more serious hobby that leads to a national title. It all depends on the personal aspirations of the individual.

If you decide to compete, you should be aware of your options. The USTRC and its producers stage three levels of events where ropers of any skill level—novice, amateur, or professional—can compete. These are sanctioned events, Regional Finals, and the National Finals.

1   More than 80 sanctioned events, also known as qualifiers, are USTRC-recognized events held each year from coast to coast, and are open to all USTRC members. These ropings qualify entrants for the other two types of competition.

2   Regional Finals are smaller-scaled versions of the pinnacle competition of the sport—the National Finals. These regional championship events were created when the USTRC realized many qualified ropers wanted to attend a premium roping closer to their home and at a more affordable cost than the National Finals.

3   The National Finals of Team Roping, or National Finals, is the premier championship event of the USTRC. It is a qualifying competition, held annually in Oklahoma City, Oklahoma.

The USTRC also *affiliates* an additional 350 to 400 events each year. These ropings are mostly smaller, local competitions that act as a feeder to the larger sanctioned events. Affiliate events do not need to adhere to the much stricter guidelines stipulated at sanctioned ropings. However, the USTRC does recognize money won at affiliate events toward qualification to enter a Regional Finals and the National Finals.

In order to participate at affiliate events, ropers are required to be a current USTRC member.

## A Worthy Goal—Earning a Shoot-Out

One of the features of the USTRC program that drew the attention of the team-roping world when it was first established was what has now become a fixture—the *Shoot-Out*.

Even though the term has become nearly as commonplace as boots and spurs in the team roping world, there are still plenty of uninitiated people who believe that a Shoot-Out is just a historical event that happened at the O.K. Corral. So, let's define it.

A Shoot-Out, in its current nomenclature, really has a double meaning. First, it is the name of a special roping division held only at a USTRC Regional Finals or at the National Finals of Team Roping. Second, it is the earned capacity to participate in one of these Shoot-Out events.

The Shoot-Out roping was created for the purpose of determining annual regional and national champions in each of the several USTRC roping divisions. The theory behind it was to bring the best teams from all over the country together and let them compete against each other to determine the best. While an entry fee is required for you to compete in a Shoot-Out, entry is not possible unless the spot has been earned through qualification. There are essentially four ways for you to earn your way there. But before discussing those four ways, integral to the process of attaining Shoot-Outs is the understanding of and distinction between Applied and Flex Earnings (points), because each can be utilized to garner Shoot-Outs.

**Applied Earnings:** Earnings a roper acquires as a result of placing at approved USTRC sanctioned and/or affiliate events. Earnings can be carried over from season to season.

**Flex Earnings:** Earnings a roper acquires as a direct result of placing in the Average of sanctioned (not affiliate) events. Earnings are awarded in either $2,000 or $6,000 allotments depending on how high a team finished in the Average and how many teams competed in the event's division. Earnings cannot be carried over from season to season. For example, placing first through third in the Average of a division with between 251 to 300 teams competing earns $6,000 in Flex Earnings, while placing fourth through eighth earns $2,000 in Flex Earnings for each team.

With either Applied or Flex Earnings, or a combination of the two, a roper can "purchase" (that is, qualify for) a National Finals Shoot-Out for $6,000 or a Regional Finals Shoot-Out for $2,000. With that in mind, the four ways a roper can earn Shoot-Outs are:

1   Using money earned at USTRC sanctioned and affiliate ropings (Applied Earnings).

2   Using Flex Earnings collected at sanctioned ropings.

3   Qualifying for the short round of a Preliminary Division at the Regional Finals ($2,000 Flex Earnings/team) and/or placing in the top five in the Average at a Regional Finals ($6,000 Flex Earnings/team).

4   Qualifying for the short round of a Preliminary Division at the National Finals ($6,000 Flex Earnings/team).

Shoot-Out entrance has added value because as the regular season progresses, a portion of each roper's fees are placed in a pool called the Shoot-Out Fund. This is different than the traditional jackpot format and it serves to significantly increase the payout when the Shoot-Out competition is held. I'll explain how:

If you remember, team roping is a pay-to-play sport. That is, at a typical event, you put your money up to enter and it all goes into the collective "pot." After the expenses of putting on the competition are covered, the remainder is paid out to the winning teams.

With this conventional scenario, the only way a roping can pay out increased money is to enter additional teams. That is, unless there is some sort of supplementary, added payback source. In the case of the Shoot-Out, the USTRC provides this additional flow of cash for its sanctioned events via its Shoot-Out Fund.

The money in the USTRC's Shoot-Out Fund is made up of 5 percent of the purses from all of that season's sanctioned events; 1.7 percent in contributions from each roping producer's commission; added Affiliate event funding; and some sponsorship monies. When these sources are combined, the total amount of money accumulated in the Fund can be considerable. The Shoot-Out Fund for the 2009 Cinch National Finals of Team Roping, for instance, was more than $1.3 million.

At that same championship event, the money added to each division ranged from $73,750 for each of the Gold Plus Shoot-Outs to $170,000 for the #11 Shoot-Out. Every Shoot-Out at the 2009 Finals except the #8 division paid more than $80,000 to the winning team, with $108,400 going to the winning team in the #10 Shoot-Out. Combine those dollars with the fact that only a limited number of teams qualify to enter a Shoot-Out and you can understand these events' considerable worth.

## THE AVERAGE JOE OR JILL

Who is the face of USTRC? What does its membership look like? Just who is a team roper? Well, the profile of a modern competitor might surprise you.

While many roping competitors still hone their skills on traditional Western ranches, most today do not. For the vast majority, this fact is not a handicap. Rather, it may be a blessing, especially if they have quality instruction from the beginning that helps them sidestep a bad habit or two.

Until recently, team roping has been a predominantly male-dominated sport, with more than 85 percent of USTRC members being men. But that percentage is changing. Lately, more and more females are discovering the attraction of the sport, the fun, the thrill, and the competition (fig. 1.4).

*1.4 Although team roping has traditionally been a male-dominated sport, today women are a fast-growing part of the USTRC's membership. In fact, there are a number of all female events now, including the National Finals Cruel Girl Championships.*

At least two factors are contributing to this trend. The first is the classification system itself, which allows beginners of any age to start competing in the sport at an introductory level. The second is a relatively recent shift by youth rodeo associations to encourage girls to compete in a wider variety of rodeo sports, team roping being one of these events. Also, in this era of athletic equality, young girls do not encounter the "gender stigma" toward team roping that had sometimes impacted previous generations.

Today's team ropings are often peppered with women competing as teammates with both men and women. In fact, there are a number of all female events now, including the National Finals Cruel Girl Championships.

In addition to its incentives for women, the USTRC has taken some proactive steps to ensure there will be competitors in the future. For example, youth memberships are free to those under the age of 12 and include a wide array of benefits—from competition privileges that reward winners with scholarships and big-ticket prizes, to everyday entertainment items like roping-themed coloring books and stickers.

Although children of all ages may compete on live cattle, the USTRC holds a special competition designed for those who hold youth membership cards, which lets them practice their skills in a safe and controlled environment. Known as *dummy roping*, children attempt to rope a plastic or other type of molded steer head—the dummy—around the head or horns (fig. 1.5). The event's rules are modeled after the live competition guidelines, as are the significant prizes and incentives that are awarded to the champions. (You can learn more about competitive dummy roping for children in chapter 5, p. 90.)

Although the sport of team roping is becoming more popular with both women and youth, it is still predominantly made up of 25- to 54-year-old males who own horses and live in rural or suburban areas. While many of this demographic are connected in some way with the farming or ranching industries, the majority hails from other walks of life and may be teachers,

1.5 *Junior Looper members are eligible to enter a competition designed just for them, called dummy roping. Here, a boy throws a loop during such an event.*

plumbers, firemen, salesmen, or businessmen. Their ranks, like any segment of the USTRC's membership, include anyone who is fascinated with the Western lifestyle—the attitudes, ethics, and history of the American cowboy culture.

What better way to tap into that culture than gallop horseback after a steer, rope in hand?

## GETTING STARTED

Many enthusiasts have realized the benefits and excitement of competing as a team roper. But, what skills and resources does the sport require? How does a beginner get started? Or, how can an amateur roper take the right steps to improve?

The answers to these questions are the heart of what this book seeks to address with the help of a few industry experts and everyday ropers. It will take you from being a spectator in the stands to the roping box, with guidance every step of the way.

# 2

# ROPING EQUIPMENT

LIKE ANY SPORT, TEAM ROPING comes with its own set of equipment requirements. A peek into any competitor's bag reveals not just the expected ropes but a variety of other gear designed to make him faster, better, or safer. An enthusiast's shopping list may also include a few other items—everything from the staple practice dummy to the latest high-tech training tools. Read on to learn more about the equipment that can make or break a roper's run.

## ROPES

No roper can exist without them, yet ropes can cause much confusion for beginners. Step into any Western tack shop and you are sure to be greeted with several varieties of brightly hued options that all claim to be the one that will take you to the pay window (fig. 2.1). So, how do you decide which one is really right for you? First, I'll take a step back to investigate the beginnings of the modern team rope.

Equibrand® is a leading corporation that is known for producing top-quality tack and equipment for a variety of equine disciplines, including team roping. It is the latest generation of a company that began as Classic Ropes, a

modest rope manufacturer tucked away in the small Texas town of Granbury. In the modern rope market, Classic first found its way to the limelight with a bright green model that was appropriately named the MoneyMaker®. It was the first lariat to combine nylon with polyester. Previously, nylon was the only option.

Polyester is a heavier fiber than nylon. Its added weight helps the roper feel what the different parts of the rope are doing throughout the swing, throw, and catch.

However, nylon is still the predominate fiber in modern team-roping ropes because it is flexible and it stretches. Stretch allows for different *lays* (stiffness) in ropes. The different

*2.1 Modern ropes come in a rainbow of colors. Each hue signals a rope's use and material blend. Although it may be intimidating choosing that first rope, this chapter walks you through you options.*

lays that nylon helps to provide allow each roper to select the feel that's right for him. And, when nylon fibers are twisted together, they give the rope body, which helps the loop stay open when delivering it to the target.

Blending these two materials has its own advantages. The main one is that it allows manufacturers to pack more weight into a smaller diameter of rope, which gives users more control when it is in motion.

Among the ropes manufactured by Equibrand, five basic nylons and three basic polyesters are combined in different ways to make a variety of ropes. Each blend is formulated according to factors like seasonal temperatures, the stiffness needed, or the rope's intended use.

In addition to revamping the recipe for a great rope, Equibrand also employed a modern waxing process, which condensed the timeframe it took to produce a finished product. Previously, ropes required aging for months outdoors in the sun before they were properly treated and ready for competition. With today's twisting and waxing processes, a rope can be made one day and ready to use the next.

Blends also opened the door for color variations. One reason for this was that outdoor elements were no longer involved in the manufacturing process, which gave each rope the same tan hue. Also, new polyester materials influenced how a rope looked through the dyes used.

Color entered the team roping market by accident. A rainbow palette first made its debut when rope-makers utilized colored polyester fibers from the tire and carpet industries. As polyester became a component of their ropes, the tint of the poly fiber transformed the rope's appearance with vibrant colorations. However, mere happenstance is not the case when selecting colors today. Dyes are carefully chosen to differentiate each type of rope from other styles and brands, and are applied quite deliberately (fig. 2.2).

As mentioned, most modern team roping competition ropes are coated in heated wax soon after manufacture to add to their life and durability, preserve greater color, and provide a cleaner look.

## Diagram of a Rope

Every rope has a few standard parts and ropers should be familiar with all of them (figs. 2.3 A–F). Here is a quick review:

**Eye (hondo):** The *eye* is at one end of the rope and forms a small loop that the rest of the rope threads through.

2.2 *Ropes used to be a uniform tan hue, due to their manufacturing process, which called for months of aging outdoors. Then, polyester fibers were introduced, which not only sped up the timetable of creation, but also yielded many colors. Here, a red dye is being added to rope fibers to help distinguish a specific brand of rope from other models.*

**Burner:** The leather or rawhide patch sewn on the end of the eye is called the *burner*. A burner prevents the rope from wearing through the eye and makes the rope slide faster, because drag is reduced. A burner should last the lifetime of the rope.

**Tail:** Opposite of the eye, the other end of the rope terminates in a knot called the *tail*.

**Loop:** When the tail is passed through the eye, a circle of rope (the *loop*) is formed. Properly sized, this is what the roper actually swings around his head and throws to catch a steer. Correct loop size is different for each roper; however, beginners should have larger loops than more experienced ropers. As a general rule, a loop's diameter should be the distance from a hand outstretched at shoulder height to the ground.

**Tip:** When the loop is swung, the *tip* is the point farthest from the roper. Centrifugal force will give a tip weight, similar to a person swinging a bucket of water: The same way the water doesn't slosh from the bucket because the force keeps it in, the tip also pushes out with weight away from the roper during the swing.

**Spoke:** The area of the loop between the eye and the hand that grasps the loop. The *spoke* consists of two strands of rope—top and bottom. A lot of novice ropers grab their loop's spoke close to the eye, which doesn't give them

2.3 A–F *Equibrand's Chief Operating Officer Craig Bray demonstrates the proper way to hold a rope (A). His company is a major manufacturer of team roping gear. The small opening at one end of the rope is called the eye, or hondo (B). The rest of the rope slips through this to make the loop, which is what is used to catch a steer. A leather burner prevents friction from wearing away at the eye, which extends the rope's life. At the opposite end from the eye, the rope terminates in the tail, which is a knot that prevents the rope from unraveling (C). The loop is the part of a rope that a team roper actually swings in his hand and throws to catch a steer's horns or heels (D). The part of the loop that a roper holds is called the spoke. It has two parts, or strands. A roper should hold the spoke at least 2 feet from the eye (E). Excess rope should be wound neatly into coils, which are held by the same hand that holds the bridle rein (F).*

much control over the tip. At least 2 feet of spoke gives you more balance. A good guideline to remember is that when you are holding your loop, ideally the eye should be about halfway between the tip of the loop and your hand.

**Coils:** Excess rope between the loop and the tail is gathered neatly into one hand (the one *not* swinging the loop) by rolling it into manageable circles called *coils*.

## Purchasing a Rope

### Length and Diameter

The are a few basic considerations when you decide to purchase a rope. For example, take length. As a general rule, professionals in the industry recommend that all *headers* use a 30-foot rope and all *heelers* a 35-foot one (fig. 2.4).

Ropes also come in a variety of diameters, which are measured in fractions of an inch. In order of increasing width, typical diameters in inches include: 3/16, 5/16, 5/16 *full*, 3/8 *scant*, 3/8, 3/8 *full*, 7/16 *scant*, 7/16, and 7/16 *full*. *Scant* simply refers to the fact that a rope's diameter is slightly smaller than the standard measurement, while *full* means it is a bit thicker.

The two most popular diameter options for team ropers today are the 3/8 inch *scant* and a true 3/8 inch size. However, it is ultimately up to each individual roper to decide the thickness that feels right for him.

2.4 *The manufacture of these ropes is finished, except for cutting them to length. Length is determined by who will use them. Headers need 30-foot long ropes, whereas heelers need at least 35 feet in length.*

### Lay (Stiffness)

Generally, softer ropes are recommended for beginner headers and heelers, because they are easier to handle. More limber types also make it easier for you when you are learning to *dally,* or wrap the rope around your horn. However, stiffer ropes do have advantages, such as their increased ability to hold the loop open in the swing and throw.

Typical *lay* (stiffness) options include double extra-soft; extra-soft; soft, medium soft; medium; hard medium; medium hard; and hard. A new header should start out with a 30-foot double extra-soft or extra-soft, whereas a heeler should begin with a 35-foot soft or medium-soft. Heelers need a stiffer rope because their loop needs to land on the ground and stay wide open for the steer's hind feet to step into (fig. 2.5). While a stiffer rope will help keep a loop open, these ropes are more difficult to control when swinging and aiming a throw.

2.5  *Heelers need a stiffer rope because their loop needs to stay wide open for the steer's hind feet to step into. However, while a stiffer rope helps keep a loop open, these ropes are more difficult to control when swinging and aiming a throw. That is why new ropers are cautioned against getting ropes that are too stiff.*

As a heeler progresses in skill, after six to eight months of practice, roping instructors generally recommend moving to a medium-soft lay. Ultimately, he should advance to using a medium rope.

## Strands

You can also choose the *number of strands* in a rope. The use of this term is not to be confused with the strands that make up the *spoke of a loop*. In this case, strand refers to the twisted groups of fibers that make up the rope.

Your options include three-, four-, and five-strand ropes. More strands amplify everything within the loop, which makes it easier to swing, more forgiving, and more consistent because there is more weight packed into a smaller diameter.

Four- and five-strand ropes operate around an axis and are wound tighter than three-strand versions. This means temperature variances don't affect performance.

Three-strand ropes, on the other hand, are affected by the climate. This is because scorching or frigid weather changes how loosely or tightly a rope's fibers are wound. This means the same rope can swing and throw differently from summer to winter. However, adjustments to the manufacturing process ensures that a warm-weather rope feels consistent with a cold-weather rope, providing they are used in the proper months.

Four- and five-strands also give more weight to the tip of the loop when you are swinging it, making the tip easier to feel and the loop easier to throw. That can increase consistency—and catch ratios—because you can feel the loop better. More strands also lend additional body to a loop, helping prevent it from collapsing. This means that even if you don't have a perfect swing, a loop with more strands gives you a greater tendency to stay open.

Another tip for a first-time buyer is to start out with a heavier rope—which makes it easier to feel each of the parts as they move—and then progress to lighter versions. One cautionary note is to be careful to avoid a rope that is too heavy, as it may cause fatigue.

## Pre-Purchase Exams

**Kick:** Test-swinging the rope in the store is highly recommended. One feature you should make sure to investigate is *kick*. Kick is a built-in aid that every good rope has to help a roper swing their loop and keep that loop open when it is thrown. Every manufacturer strives to create perfect kick in their ropes. Fortunately for beginners, it is easy to check this feature and most retailers encourage customers to test their ropes in the store.

To test a prospective rope's kick, take the rope out of the package. With either hand, drop the first coil, or loop, straight down. The eye (hondo) at

2.6 *This new rope demonstrates proper kick. Notice that the dropped loop falls at about a 90-degree angle to the rest of the coils.*

the end of the rope should automatically rotate—or kick—itself from that straight position to one that is turned approximately 90 degrees to the rest of the coils (fig. 2.6). Most novice team ropers need the full degree of kick, because it helps them swing.

New ropers should never buy a rope without kick, where the dropped loop just lines up "straight" to the front. Only advanced competitors, who have the talent and control to handle ropes tied in this fashion, should consider purchasing one. Novice and intermediate ropers should save their money and avoid a future of frustrated performances by buying a rope with more forgiving kick.

**Eye Placement:** A second, quick, in-store test when shopping for a rope is to check the eye, simply by swinging the rope as if you were actually going to catch something. (Learn to properly swing a rope starting on p. 84 in chapter 5.) Ideally, the eye should maintain the same position—centered on the strands, lying flat and straight—during the motion of the swing as it had when still.

However, don't be confused by eye placement when you see some new ropes on the store shelf or rack. While three-strand ropes are usually displayed with a properly-placed "straight" eye, four- and five-strand ropes—which are made with a different twisting process—are often packaged with the eye preset to the right. Their manufacturing process predisposes them to rotate left, back to their natural state. A manufacturer packages the eye differently, so it will perform perfectly when you take it home. The first time you use one of these four- or five-strand ropes, swinging it will set the eye to the correct placement.

A closely-related bit of advice examines the proper position of the top strand in relation to the eye. When selecting a rope, make sure that the top strand exits the eye on the offside of the eye's knot. This helps the rope slide smoothly, because the knot isn't interfering with movement (fig. 2.7).

Once purchased, you can keep your rope in good working order by being careful how you put it away. Correct storage helps to "train" the rope's parts, particularly the eye. To maintain proper form, coil your rope evenly using big coils, and make sure the eye is straight before placing the rope in your rope bag. To avoid the eye being turned while in the rope bag, place your rope so that the eye is at the top of the bag. Next, store the rope bag in an upright position in a cool, dry place.

## Ropes for Youth

While many youth use adult ropes, manufacturers make several models for kids. Some of these are not meant to catch live cattle, but others are simply scaled-down versions of the full-sized adult performance ropes. For many youth competitors, team roping is not merely "child's play"—they need gear tough enough to do the job.

Child ropes start as small as 3/16-inch diameter and 15 feet long for the tiniest junior roper. From these "toys," many kids advance to a 1/4-inch diameter, 22-foot-long model when they are ready to begin dummy roping. Young ropers can start turning steers with a 3/8-inch by 30-foot rope, which is also a size adult ranchers find good for tasks out on the range. Young heelers, however, need to use one of the smaller adult ropes that are 35-foot long. Heelers need the extra length to reach a steer's hind feet from horseback, and the extra weight of a longer rope helps place their loop.

## ROPE BAG

The purchase of a rope necessitates the purchase of a *rope bag* that protects your rope and provides a simple storage option (fig. 2.8). You can pick from a variety of styles and colors that range from sedate earth tones to trendy prints encrusted in "bling." Wherever you end up in the spectrum, select a bag that has more than one area to put your ropes into, with dividers to keep them separate. Another option worth consideration is a bag that has a mesh pocket on the outside to hold dirty or muddy ropes.

Interior storage areas of your rope bag should be constructed of solid fabric. Ropes can be left dusted with rope powder (which I discuss on p. 40), and the ability to keep these ropes separate prevents this dust from drifting to unwanted areas.

Select a rope bag that is made from durable, thick materials with strong nylon handles. Tug on the fabric a bit and check the stitching with an eye for hardy fabrics and quality construction.

The rope bag will be home not only to ropes, but your other miscellaneous gear, competition paperwork, and horse records. With these in mind,

2.7 *When choosing a new rope, investigate how the eye's knot is placed in relation to the top strand. Ideally, a rope's top strand should exit the eye on the offside of the knot.*

2.8 *Rope bags come in all styles, sizes, and colors, so you are sure to find one that suits your tastes. Here is a typical selection, from classic solid colors to trendy animal prints. Also featured is a child's bag, which is smaller and has shoulder straps so it can be carried on the back.*

*2.9 Roping gloves are a must-have for any team roper. Usually worn only on the hand that is swinging the loop, it is unsafe to rope without one. There are two basic material options for roping gloves: cotton (left) or synthetic (right). While cotton is more economical, synthetic materials are more durable.*

*2.10 All team roping ropes are waxed in the manufacturing process. While this offers many benefits, the wax can make a rope sticky to touch. To counter this, manufacturers apply powder. Eventually, this powder can wear thin, which is why every roper needs to have their own powder on hand.*

most bags feature compartments to accommodate these items.

Child rope bags are built for the smaller, junior ropes. Because children's ropes aren't as big, the bags are scaled down accordingly. Also, many are backpack models, with enough storage compartments for them to pull double-duty, holding school supplies as well as roping equipment.

## GLOVES

One of the most essential pieces of gear for a roper is a glove. A roper typically just wears one glove on the hand that swings the loop (fig. 2.9). The purpose of a glove is twofold. It keeps your hand from getting burned should you lose control of the rope, and it makes the rope feel slicker, so it runs through your hand more easily.

You have two basic options when it comes to gloves—cotton and synthetic materials. Cotton is the more economical; synthetic the more durable and it offers more protection. Your decision is a matter of personal preference.

Finding the right size for your new glove is easy. Like street gloves, roping gloves come in standard sizes—small, medium, and large. Also, tack shops often have open packages of each, so you can try them out. A main consideration is not to get one that it overly large, which will wrinkle and possibly injure your hand.

## ROPE POWDER

As mentioned earlier, you might need to apply rope powder to your ropes (fig. 2.10). When a team roping rope is made, it is dipped in hot, liquid wax, which then hardens around it. While the wax helps bind the fibers of the rope together, it also makes the rope sticky to touch. To counter this and to make a rope move more smoothly, a manufacturer dusts powder on the finished product.

2.11 *Every roper needs a stationary dummy to practice on. While many are geared toward headers or heelers specifically, this model offers a target for both types of ropers. Note the horn wrap on the head, which helps give a rope grip on an otherwise slippery surface. It serves a different purpose on live cattle, where the wrap is primarily for the steer's protection.*

Over time, the manufacturer's powder can wear thin. Powder can be purchased separately, so you can reapply some as needed. While you can buy specially designed powder for this purpose, talc, baby powder, or cornstarch make cost-effective substitutes.

## STATIONARY PRACTICE DUMMIES

Once your rope bag is fully stocked, it is time to load up on educational gear. One essential item is the *practice dummy*. An artificial steer head or set of heels doesn't need to be extravagant, but you do need something to practice catching (fig. 2.11). A heeler can start out with a dummy that is as rudimentary as a saw horse. A header needs something a bit more realistic, but still can begin by roping a basic stationary target—such as a set of rawhide horns stuck in a bale of hay.

*2.12 This is a typical mechanical steer, which is pulled behind a motorized vehicle. Many models incorporate lifelike movement when they are in motion, making them an ideal transition tool between stationary dummies and live cattle.*

There are a variety of manufactured models to choose from as well; however, for beginners, it's especially important that plastic steer heads have a *horn wrap*—the head protection that live cattle wear while they are being roped—in order to give something for the rope to grip onto. (You can read more about roping dummies beginning on p. 89 in chapter 5.)

## MECHANICAL STEERS

Mechanical practice steers are essentially full-body dummies that incorporate movement, so a rider can learn to rope from horseback. They are often used as the transition between roping a stationary dummy and a live steer (fig. 2.12). The importance of mechanical steers is reviewed at length in chapter 7, beginning on p. 111.

## A DIGITAL AGE

The newest learning tools are available for you to use in the comfort of your own climate-controlled home. The Internet has opened many doors for sharing knowledge on many subjects, and team roping is no exception. Many professionals are finding it a great way to educate the public.

The variety and breadth of team roping aids on the market today are astounding—not the least of which are the increasing number of websites devoted to the subject that are currently popping up on the Internet. The instant access to the knowledge that the Internet provides has had a phenomenal affect on the recent growth of the sport.

Sites such as www.speedroping.com offer videos geared toward ropers who are rated 3s, 4s and 5s to show them how experts like eight-time world champion Speed Williams trains and practices. Fellow champion, professional team roper, and instructor Rickey Green's website, www.powerteamroping.com, features video tutorials and a blog, where visitors can directly ask the educator questions.

Learning how to team rope, while not excessively difficult, is not something you can learn in just a few outings. Rickey Green cautions newcomers against purchasing their equipment and heading straight out to the nearest competition before they've spent significant time in the practice arena (fig. 2.13).

In addition to learning about the sport from others, Speed Williams is a firm believer in ropers learning from themselves. He advises turning the cameras on you during training, and has always had someone film him. Williams also shoots videos of each of his students.

2.13 *Professional team roper and instructor Rickey Green has coached amateurs to success for three decades. You can learn more about Green at his website, www. powerteamroping.com.*

## ADDED OPTIONS

The tools listed in this chapter are only a few of the wide variety of options available to the modern roper. Some of the innovative tools to make the learning and competitive experiences better didn't exist a few years ago. Today, you can choose to purchase anything from the time-honored, basic gear to the ultra trendy, whichever your tastes dictate.

# TACK

T EAM ROPING IS ALL-INCLUSIVE when it comes to how your horse is outfitted. While some other riding events stress tack that is laden with expensive silver or decoration, this sport emphasizes practical, working gear.

The first thing to think about with any piece of tack is safety. The second is comfort for both you and your horse. Good looks should follow these two considerations.

Although Western tack may all seem the same at first glance, team roping has tailored the basic saddles, bridles, and other equipment for the sport's particular needs. Some of those modifications are essential for a roper to perform well, and are therefore important to know about (figs. 3.1 A & B).

## SADDLES

Your horse is one of the most significant investments you will make in your

3.1 A & B *This fully-tacked team roping horse (seen from two angles) displays the "roping tack necessities" we discuss in this chapter—properly fit and adjusted.*

sport. Ensuring that your saddle fits him properly is a simple step toward protecting this important asset (fig. 3.2). Unfortunately, some team roping horses suffer from discomfort caused by a saddle not shaped correctly to their back. When you ride in an improperly fitted saddle, it causes pain throughout the horse's body. A badly designed saddle could cause a *pressure point*, which not only leads to soreness at that one spot, but every muscle attached to that area. This can include not only the tissue along the spine, but the muscles in the neck and the hip (fig. 3.3). Pain due to a poorly fitting saddle can cause a bad or even dangerous performance, so it only makes sense to find the right saddle for your horse.

For all Western saddles, a general rule for checking fit is to be sure the forward-most *concho*—the often decorative leather or silver disks, or D-rings found in several places on the side of the saddle—is *behind* the horse's scapula (shoulder blade). This area of the horse is easy to locate: There is a distinct groove as the shoulder joins the barrel—or midsection—of the horse.

56

Team Roping 101

B

Tack

3.2 *Team roping saddles have made several modifications to the basic Western saddle design, including a substantially larger horn and cinches, which can take the tug of a large steer.*

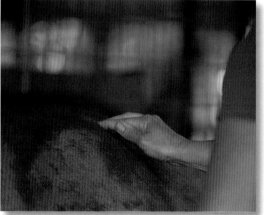

3.3 *Poorly-fitted saddles can cause pain or injury, which can show up in places like the soft tissue of a horse's back. Here, a sports massage therapist checks the tender withers of a sore horse.*

3.4 *Team roping saddle seats are generally shorter than in saddles used in most other Western disciplines. That is because in this sport, riders spend most of their run sitting farther forward, as shown here.*

Here's another tip: Pay attention to *dry spots* on your horse's back when you take the saddle off after a ride. If you notice dry spots when the rest of the back is damp with sweat, or if you find the presence of white hairs on the back of a solid-colored horse, these may indicate areas with pressure points that need to be dealt with. Test fit by placing your saddle on your horse's back without any pads. Then, lay your palm flat under the gullet of the saddle and run your fingers down the length of your horse's back. If you are able to move your hand smoothly all the way without it feeling pinched, the fit is probably decent. If not, it means there is likely a problem with how the shape of the saddle is accommodating (or not) the horse's back shape, which may cause the horse to buck or stop awkwardly. (Find out about saddle-fit solutions in the section of this chapter dealing with padding, beginning on p. 50.)

Making sure a saddle is comfortable for your horse is only half the equation. Saddle fit for the rider is equally important. However, sizing a saddle seat for a team roper is a bit unique in that team roping saddles typically have a shorter seat than saddles for other Western events. The roper's movement is shifted farther forward, and a shorter seat helps keep you in position. Equibrand's most popular sizes for team ropers are 14.5 inches to 15.5 inches—even for larger riders. Too long of a seat may cause you to be thrown back out of position, which impedes your ability to compete. It's harder to establish a proper body position in a seat that is too large (fig. 3.4).

A custom feature found on a team roping saddle is its specialized horn. Present on all Western saddles, the horn holds a far greater purpose in this sport than just something to grip if you lose your balance. It is vital to the success of a team roping run, and must be strong to withstand the pull of large steers. Typically, a team roping horn is 3.5 to 4 inches high, with a horn cap at least 3 inches in diameter to hold the *dally* in place (fig. 3.5).

## Saddle Accessories

Once the saddle is selected and fit properly, it is time to make a few decisions about the accessories that accompany it. Much like purchasing a vehicle, your saddle can come with the standard fittings and accessories, or you can upgrade to high performance versions of these items. What you choose is entirely up to you, and deciding what you want is part of the fun. Whatever you decide to garnish your saddle with, it is important to know the function and features of each piece. Here are a few of the most common ones.

### *Saddle Pad*

The padding you place between your horse and the saddle can have a major effect on your horse's performance. Even a well-fitted saddle can be uncomfortable when the wrong pad is used. This is why the pad should be one of your first considerations after finding the right saddle.

Once proper placement of the saddle on the horse's back is achieved, there should be an additional 2 or 3 inches of pad length in front of the saddle's skirts. This ensures long enough padding under the saddle during the ride, even if it shifts a little because of the horse's motion (fig. 3.6).

Another important dimension to consider for a saddle pad is thickness. If a saddle is fitted properly, a 3/4-inch to 1-inch depth is adequate. Less padding might not provide enough cushioning. Extra thickness can make a saddle shift and roll, meaning the rider must cinch his horse up more tightly to secure the saddle. This can cause soreness in the horse's belly area.

A good indication that you have the proper pad thickness is to place your fingers at the front of the saddle, between the top of the pad and underneath the saddle's gullet, which is directly below the horn. Two or three fingers should fit in this space (fig. 3.7). If you have an especially high-withered horse, a pad with cut outs or that has been notched in the wither area can help ensure fit.

While many styles exist, any good saddle pad is soft and flexible, yet still maintains enough density to absorb shock from the motions of riding. Although pads are created from many different materials, professionals recommend that all team roping pads include a natural material called *wool felt* as a component. The percentage of this product included and how it is incorporated may change

3.5 *A team roping saddle's horn is significantly larger and of more rugged construction than most Western saddle horns because it must withstand the tug of a steer.*

3.7 *Make sure there is at least two or three fingers-width of space between the bottom of the saddle's gullet and the top of the saddle pad. That allowance will prevent any painful pinching on your horse's withers during the ride.*

3.6 *As illustrated here, check that your pad extends 2 or 3 inches in front of the saddle skirts when your horse is saddled. The extra length ensures ample coverage throughout an active run, even if the pad shifts a bit as your horse moves.*

3.8 *Roping saddles have two cinches, both significantly wider than on standard Western saddles to help distribute pressure when the steer pulls on the rope.*

3.9 *The front cinch provides most of the grip to keep the saddle in place. Most team ropers are advised to use a mohair or mohair-blend front cinch, like this one, because natural materials stretch slightly, allowing a horse to take deep breaths as he runs.*

between models, but it should be present in some form. Wool felt has the ability to breathe and is a great shock absorber. There are some higher-tech materials that can also absorb shock, but wool felt's inherent benefits are hard to beat.

Whatever type of padding you choose, the best step you can take to keep it working properly is to keep it clean. Not only is a hard and crusty pad unattractive, it can also make a horse sore. So, remember to wash or brush dirt and debris off regularly. Sometimes, manufacturers include maintenance instructions with the packaging of a new pad.

### Cinch

Cinch. Girth. Whatever you call it, every saddle has one, and roping saddles should have two (fig. 3.8). The cinch wraps around the belly of a horse like a belt and secures the saddle on the horse's back. It is adjusted once the saddle and pad are in place.

3.10 *The back cinch should be snug to the horse's belly, especially during the run. If the back cinch is loose when a steer is caught and dallied to the horn, the back of the saddle could rise off the horse's back, amplifying the pressure on the horse's withers.*

Both front and back team roping cinches are generally several inches wider than the average Western cinch. The front cinch provides most of the grip to keep a saddle in place (fig. 3.9). The back cinch is dramatically wider than typical, and should be at least 7 inches across. The reason for the extra width (for both front and back) is because they need to be cinched significantly tighter than for other Western sports to prevent saddle slippage once the rope is dallied and the saddle is anchoring the weight of the steer. A larger cinch distributes that force over a greater surface area, making it more comfortable for the horse to bear.

While many ropers don't tighten their back cinches snugly, professionals say they should, because once the dally is made, the pressure is all on the saddle horn (fig. 3.10). This action makes the back part of the saddle rise off the horse's back, amplifying the pressure on the saddle's bars at the front, near the horse's withers. However, ropers should remember to loosen back cinches when work is done to give the horse a chance to relax.

Gradually tighten any cinch, rather than adjusting it with one quick jerk. This allows a horse time to get used to the idea of being saddled. It can also prevent crankiness and bad manners in the future during saddling time.

**Two Rules When Purchasing:** Where to begin when choosing a cinch? Fortunately, it's not that difficult to navigate the choices and find the right one for you. Front cinches, especially, come in many sizes and varieties, but there are only two easy rules you need to know before shopping for one:

1   When the front cinch is pulled tight, the small, metal ring located in the middle of the cinch should lie in the center of the horse's barrel just behind the horse's front legs. Conveniently, this usually lines up with the groove between the muscles in the horse's front legs.

    Proper placement of this ring is important so that any equipment running between the horse's legs and clipped to the ring—like a breast collar or a tie-down (see p. 57)—does not get close enough to either inner leg to create a sore.

2   When tightened, the D-rings on each end of the front cinch should be high enough on the horse's belly to allow free movement of the horse's elbow.

**Cinch Materials:** Choosing the elements that construct your front cinch is also simple. A few of the most common include *synthetic neoprene, natural mohair,* or a *mohair blend*. The right choice depends largely on your where you live and personal preference.

Advantages to *neoprene* are that it is anti-microbial and anti-fungal, which is great for people who live in a hot, humid climate. However, never use a nylon or neoprene cinch with nylon latigos—the straps that attach a cinch to the saddle—because it does not stretch when the horse breathes deeply. This is why *mohair* or *mohair-blend* cinches and leather latigos are recommended for most. Even when drawn tight, both components have some flexibility and "give" for the horse's comfort. This ability to stretch is also why leather is commonly used for back cinches.

**Keeper:** A final consideration with cinches is the small buckled strap, or *keeper,* that connects the front cinch to the back cinch. It runs along the midline of the horse's belly, and attaches from the front cinch's rear-facing center ring to the corresponding front-facing center ring on the back cinch.

Sometimes overlooked or adjusted improperly, the keeper prevents the back cinch from moving too close to the horse's flank. A "crawling" back cinch can irritate a horse and cause him to buck. Made of leather or another smooth, strong material, a keeper should be no longer than 2 or 3 inches.

*Breast Collar*

While horses in many Western events get along just fine without them, breast collars are essential for team roping. When a steer pulls on the saddle's horn, a breast collar helps keep the saddle centered on the horse's back. It also gives the horse something to push against during the run, much like a harness collar for a driving horse (fig. 3.11).

When adjusting a breast collar, make sure it covers from the center of the chest toward the saddle above each of the horse's shoulders. Too loose and low, it can impede your horse's stride, sometimes even tripping him. Too tight, when your horse extends his legs, it can pull the saddle into his shoulder blades. At best, this can shorten your horse's stride, and at worst, cause pain.

Another consideration when fitting the breast collar is the *tug*, the part that runs from the center of the chest down between the horse's front legs and ends where it clips to the foremost center ring of the front cinch. Keep in mind that although you are saddling your horse when he is standing still, you need to adjust each part of your breast collar for when he is running at full speed. For example, when attaching the tug, allow enough length so that your horse can move his shoulders freely. If the tug is tight when he is standing still, it will be extremely so when the horse tries to gallop (fig. 3.12).

One detail that shouldn't be forgotten on a breast collar used for team roping is a *tie-down keeper* (fig. 3.13). This small loop of leather or other flexible material provides a safe way to *tuck* the tie-down—a strap that runs from the horse's head and between his front legs to the foremost center ring of the front cinch—close to his body. If allowed to flop loose, the tie-down could trip up a horse and cause significant injuries to all involved. (You'll learn more about tie-downs on p. 57.)

3.11 *A breast collar works like a harness collar, giving the horse something to push against. It also helps stabilize the saddle.*

3.12 *Allow room when adjusting the breast collar to allow your horse a free range of motion. What might appear to fit properly when he is standing still may be too tight when he is extended into a full gallop. On the other hand, a breast collar that is too loose can trip a horse in motion. Make sure yours is in-between.*

3.13 *The tie-down keeper is a small loop of leather or other flexible material that provides a safe way to tuck a tie-down—the strap that runs from the roping horse's head down between his front legs—close to his body. If allowed to flop loose, the tie-down could trip up a horse and cause significant injuries to all involved.*

## Dally Rubber

A team roping saddle horn has its own specialized accessory—*dally rubber* (see fig. 3.5, p. 51). This circle of flexible material resembles an oversized rubber band, and it serves a couple of purposes. First, it prevents rope from slipping on the horn when a roper dallies. Also, it protects the horn from rope burns should the rope slip.

There should be several layers of rubber on the horn to provide the needed cushion. The outermost layer of wraps should be looser than the inside ones to give more grip to a dallied rope. Too soft a wrap could cause the rope to pop off the horn when you dally. A too-hard wrap will not grip the rope, making dallying more difficult.

When selecting dally rubber, ropers have two basic options—*black* and *white* (fig. 3.14). Each has its own advantages and disadvantages, and your choice depends on what features are important to you.

*Black rubber* is the most popular—produced from tire inner tubes. It is also the most economical choice. When a rope slides on black rubber, the rubber may tear, but it won't crumble—so it lasts a long time. The major drawback to this rubber is its tendency to leave black marks on clothing.

*White rubber*, which is made of a dryer, more brittle material, eliminates that issue. It does not leave marks. It also provides greater grip to your rope to help your dally hold. However, the same properties that lend it these advantages also make it prone to its main disadvantage—"shattering." When a rope slides on white rubber, it doesn't tear like black rubber, instead, it disintegrates, which means you need to replace it more often.

Whichever type you choose, keep plenty of extra dally rubber on hand. You will inevitably burn through it. If you rope with too little or none on the horn, it not only ruins the materials that make up the horn, it is unsafe. And, without it your fingers can get caught—or even cut off—in the dally.

3.14 *Dally rubber is necessary for keeping both your saddle horn in good working order and your hands safe. There are two options for these loops, which look like giant rubber bands and are twisted around a saddle horn—black and white. Seen here as they come packaged in the store, each type has its own advantages. For example, black lasts a long time, but can leave streaks of residue on clothing. White doesn't leave marks, but has a shorter lifespan.*

## TIE-DOWNS

A tie-down consists of two parts, a halter-like portion, and a strap that runs from under the chin and down between the horse's front legs to snap onto the foremost middle ring of the front cinch. Its purpose is twofold. First, it provides the horse with something to brace against while running. It is also an aid to keep the horse's body "framed" in the correct position during the high-action event (fig. 3.15).

A tie-down is not intended to be a restraint, but rather a control device that keeps the horse's head in position and helps him stay mentally focused as he works. To properly fit a tie-down strap's length, it should just be loose enough to touch the bottom of the neck when you use your hand to push it upward, while allowing the horse to maintain his natural headset (figs. 3.16 A & B).

3.15 *Tie-downs have two parts—the halter-like portion that is placed on the horse's head and the strap that runs from below the chin down between the front legs to clip onto the front cinch. Tie-downs have two purposes in team roping: They help keep horses in the right frame during high action, and they provide the horse with something to brace against when running.*

3.16 A & B *Determining the right length for your horse's tie-down is easy. It should be just long enough that you can touch the bottom of the horse's neck if you push it up (A), while allowing your horse to maintain his natural headset (B).*

Most horses perform fine with a simple, flat-leather or leather-covered rope noseband on a tie-down (fig. 3.17). More severe materials or devices are not recommended. If it seems that they are needed, you should definitely investigate the root cause of the issue, instead of simply treating the symptom. Examples of common causes could include an improperly fitted saddle, teeth that ache or are in need of floating, hock soreness, or a need for additional training. You could even have a horse that is just not physically built for the demands of team roping.

## EQUINE LEG PROTECTION

Another must-have for your shopping list is leg protection, or *boots*, for your horse. Protective boots are available in several different varieties, but they all have the same function—to prevent common injuries from occurring (fig. 3.18).

While most ropers begin to learn the sport away from their horse— and they don't need protective boots immediately—it is not a bad idea to already have them in your rope bag, waiting for you. Also, it is beneficial to allow your horse some time to get used to wearing the gear and get over any worries he may have about the boots before you ask him to perform in them.

One of the most common injuries leg protection prevents is when the hoof of one leg *clips*—or bangs—into another leg. Often, the areas affected have sensitive soft tissue, like the lower leg or the heel of a foot. A major injury can sideline a roping horse's career for an extensive amount of time.

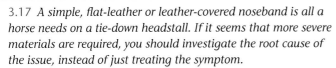

3.17 *A simple, flat-leather or leather-covered noseband is all a horse needs on a tie-down headstall. If it seems that more severe materials are required, you should investigate the root cause of the issue, instead of just treating the symptom.*

3.18 *Protective leg boots are a must-have for a high-action sport like team roping. Team roping horses may face soft-tissue strain from sudden twists and turns, or heel burn from sudden stops. Boots help prevent these injuries.*

## Front Leg Boots

Front-leg protection is essentially the same for both *heading* and *heeling* horses. Bell boots can guard the area just above the hoof on the front legs, which are susceptible to an overreaching hind hoof. Taller, wrap-type boots above the bell boot shield higher, on the inside of the horse's leg, which can be injured by a hard knock from the other front leg (fig. 3.19). Bare minimum front-leg protection should include splint boots, which protect the most vulnerable areas of the lower leg.

3.19 *This horse's front legs have complete protection with bell boots (around the ankles and back of the front hooves) and wrap-type boots (around the cannon bones and fetlocks). Bell boots guard the area just above the hoof on the front legs, which are susceptible to an overreaching hind hoof. Taller, wrap-type boots above the bell boot shield higher, on the inside of the horse's leg, which can be injured by a hard knock from the opposite front leg.*

## Hind Leg Boots

Hind-leg protection differs somewhat from that recommended for the front (fig. 3.20). *Head horses* need hind boots to prevent their fetlocks from burning against the ground when they dig into the footing while directing the steer. Taller, wrap-type boots help during the *face*, when hind legs can bump each other, damaging splint bones, tendons, and many other soft tissues.

*Heel horses* have many of the same issues, plus one—their big sliding stop. This happens when the rider is pulling the slack rope tight around the steer's hind ankles and dallying. For this maneuver, *skid boots* are a must. While leather or neoprene skid boots can be used as a stand-alone item, for maximum protection, ropers can also purchase them built into wrap-type boots that protect the cannon bone area, as well.

3.20 *This hind boot combines a tall wrap boot with a skid boot into one convenient piece of protective gear. This is especially important for heel horses—they need to have hind boots with skids, which protect them during hard, sliding stops.*

## BRIDLES

Another important piece of tack is the bridle, which consists of a few parts: the *headstall, bit, chinstrap,* and *reins.* Each part of the head gear has a specific role to play in team roping, and some are modified just for the sport.

### Headstalls

The headstall plays a supportive role on the bridle, and holds everything in place on the head. While it can be made from a variety of materials and in many different styles, proper fit is the most important consideration (fig. 3.21).

Between the horse's ears and mouth run the adjustable parts of the head-stall that are appropriately called the *cheeks.* One or both cheeks have buckles to tailor length to the individual horse's head. The most important concern with the cheeks is to make sure they are short enough so when properly fitted, they stay out of the horse's eyes.

### Bits

Bits are a confusing and often controversial topic. Some ropers use no bit, and ride instead with a mechanical hackamore, while others "hang" large amounts of "iron."

Mechanical hackamores are most effective in the hands of professionals who are riding finely tuned, responsive horses (fig. 3.22). The more commonly seen bridles have a bit that sits in the horse's mouth, over his tongue and in the space that naturally occurs between his front and back teeth.

There are generally two types of bits used in team roping: *shanked* and *non-shanked*. The *shank* is a sidepiece, a strip of metal that drops from the mouthpiece

3.21 *The headstall holds the entire bridle together and must be safe. While headstalls can be made from a variety of materials and styles, faulty or improperly fitting equipment has no place in a high-action sport like team roping.*

3.22 *A mechanical hackamore, seen here, is best used on highly-trained, responsive horses—like this 24-year-old gelding, who is very experienced at his job.*

(the *point of purchase*) to where the rein attaches. The shank may be attached to a broken (jointed) mouthpiece or a solid mouthpiece, and made with a variety of materials and methods. When buying a bit with a solid mouthpiece, you should steer away from one that is too straight, which doesn't fit the horse's mouth well and can cause discomfort. On a typical shanked roping bit, whichever mouth-piece you use, there should be one to one-and-a-half wrinkles in the corners of the horse's mouth when the cheeks are properly adjusted (fig. 3.23).

Non-shanked bits are usually *snaffles*, which come in many variations, such as the full-cheek, D-ring, or O-ring snaffle (fig. 3.24). While a snaffle bit is great for schooling a horse to keep him light and flexible, professionals discourage your using one in competition. This is because the *concave* mouthpiece could flip around, twisting painfully in the horse's mouth. A non-shanked bit also does not provide the rider the leverage needed to signal the horse at high speed.

3.24 *While snaffle bits, like the O-ring this horse is wearing, are great for schooling a horse to keep him light and flexible, they aren't the best choice for competition. This is because their concave mouthpiece could flip around, twisting painfully in the horse's mouth. Also, a non-shanked bit does not provide the rider the leverage needed to signal the horse at high speed.*

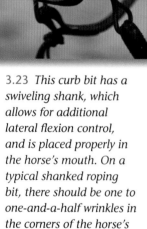

3.23 *This curb bit has a swiveling shank, which allows for additional lateral flexion control, and is placed properly in the horse's mouth. On a typical shanked roping bit, there should be one to one-and-a-half wrinkles in the corners of the horse's mouth when the cheeks are properly adjusted.*

With the advent of more mechanized manufacturing that makes a greater variety of bits available to the average consumer, be sure to search out what is best for your particular horse. Do not be swayed by fancy engraving, designs, or other visual trappings. You can get an idea of what a bit may feel like in your horse's mouth by holding it across your hand and tugging on the shanks or rings.

## Mistakes with Bitting

Ropers at all levels choose the wrong bit for their horse, but the mistakes made by beginners are often different from mistakes made at later stages. Team roping instructor Rickey Green says that the typical new roping enthusiast has a tendency to "under-bit" his horse and have a tie-down that is too loose to be effective, which causes the horse to run through the bit with his head in the air and his nose pushed out. (The beginner also tends to fit the *chin strap* too tightly—read more about properly fitting a chin strap on p. 63.)

Green adds that later on, the mid-level novice rider tends to "over-bit" his horse, as by now he may have figured out that he isn't in control. In an attempt to counter this, he goes to more severe bits to try to make his horse listen. This is where good training during everyday practice can help. If a roper can keep his horse soft in practice, it will pay off when it counts.

There is one bit often chosen inappropriately by team ropers because of its optimistic name—the *correction bit*. A type of shanked bit with a stiff port, the correction bit does have its place, just not on the horse that is fighting signals from the reins. According to Green, it actually encourages a horse to put his nose out and raise his head higher, the opposite of what most team ropers want their horse to do.

For most team roping horses, a loose shank that swivels at the *point of purchase*, or part of the bit between the mouthpiece and headstall, is a better choice. This is because it provides a degree of *lateral flexion*. A stiff bit really only gives *vertical* control.

Lateral flexion is important because team roping horses don't just travel in straight lines. They need to arc their body during a run, such as when making the left turn into the corner or when *facing*.

Ropers also should factor in the relation of the purchase to the shank. The shorter the purchase length, in relation to the shank length, the *more* leverage the bit gives the rider. When the mouthpiece is centered toward the middle of the bit, making the purchase and shank approximately the same length, the *less* leverage you have. A straighter shank lends more leverage than one that curves back toward the rider. This is because a horse feels a pull on a straight shank more quickly. A "swept-back" shank gives your horse more gradual notice.

## Chin Straps

A much-overlooked part of equipment is the *chin strap*, also referred to as a *curb strap*. Often seen as one unit with the bit, it attaches from one side of the bit to the other and lies in the groove behind the horse's chin. This small strip of leather, chain, or other material plays a big role in how a horse performs. The preferred type of strap is either made of leather, or a mild, flat chain. Using something more severe or a strap made of uncomfortable material can cause the horse to toss his head or thrust his nose out. It can even cause the horse to ignore the bit as he responds only to the pain or pressure of the chin strap.

A problem that Speed Williams and Rickey Green often see with their students is a chin strap that is fastened too tightly. When a rider picks up on the reins, the horse should first feel the cue from the bit, followed by the chin strap. When this curb strap is too tight, the horse gets a shock as both cues hit at the same time.

As mentioned earlier, a properly fitted chin strap has a space between it and the chin that three or four fingers can fit into (fig. 3.25).

## Reins

Roping reins are a unique modification to the standard split reins seen in most Western events. Although reminiscent of the English disciplines' looped rein

3.25 *As seen here, a properly fitted chin strap has a space between it and the chin that three or four fingers can fit into.*

that buckles together, roping reins are shorter and usually one solid piece. They are also held in one hand, instead of two. This is the same hand that holds the coils of your rope (fig. 3.26).

Roping reins come in many different widths, lengths, and thicknesses. A 1/2-inch to 5/8-inch is the standard, but smaller hands may require a thinner rein. Choose what feels right to you.

Reins can be constructed from many materials. For most, natural leather for both the rein and the attachments to the bit are the better choice over synthetic reins and metal snaps: Because leather stretches, the rider gets a better feel of the horse's "face" and can give a softer cue to the horse. Leather also weighs a bit more than synthetic materials, so the horse senses a quicker release when a rider drops the reins. In the case of an accident, leather reins will break faster than some synthetic materials, which can save your horse's sensitive mouth (fig. 3.27).

## FINAL THOUGHTS

It doesn't matter what the piece of tack is, our experts agree that the most important features to look for when filling your tack room are how it feels to you and how effective it is for your horse. Regardless of the price point of your purchase, their advice is to—above all—make sure it fits both of you well (fig. 3.28).

3.26 *In team roping, a rider uses a single loop rein, rather than the more common split Western reins. This is because the rider must have a hand free to swing and throw his rope. A loop rein is easier to hold in the other hand, which must also hold the rope's coils.*

Tack

3.27 *Team roping reins come in many makes and models. Seen here are flat leather, braided leather, and braided synthetic grip reins.*

3.28 *The most important considerations for the gear that fills your tack room are good fit and functionality. This tidy team roper's tack room fits that definition well.*

# HORSES

T'S EASY TO GET INTIMIDATED BY THE EQUINE TALENT available in team roping, especially if you don't have a horse or one that is trained for the sport. But, there are many options that let you dip your toe into the sport.

## FINDING THE RIGHT HORSE FOR YOU

A great first step is to borrow a trained horse from a friend. Not only is this option free, it gives you a chance to try the sport before deciding if it is right for you. However, borrowing a horse isn't without downsides, especially when the horse tends to leave the roping box too fast for a beginner, forcing you to try to control him and swing the rope at the same time. Rather than a fast horse, as a new roper, you need a seasoned horse that knows his job, is quiet in the box, and helps you to learn correctly (fig. 4.1).

If you don't have an appropriate horse available to borrow, lessons can be another valid, cost-effective option. In a controlled environment, with an experienced horse, a beginner can progress very quickly with a good teacher.

If a lesson horse is not a practical option in your area, an alternative might be to lease a trained horse (fig. 4.2). Although leasing horses is more common among the middle and professional levels in team roping, it is definitely a valid option for beginning ropers. It is also popular with parents trying to find a horse for their youth ropers.

Regardless of how you get started, most roping enthusiasts eventually do purchase a horse. However, you need to make sure you end up with one

*4.1  Beginners need horses that break smoothly and quietly from the box, like this one, rather than those that can unseat a beginner by "exploding" out.*

*4.2  A good horse is invaluable. If you don't own one, leasing or borrowing a seasoned equine partner can be a great option that is very cost-effective.*

that is right for you. When you decide to buy a horse, safety is the number-one consideration for an entry-level prospect. Finding a well-trained horse is paramount, and a beginner should not buy too much horse for his skill level. A solid training foundation and willing mind is always important for all roping prospects, even at the professional levels.

One common mistake beginners make is to spend too much money on their first horse. While finished, reliable horses can and do come with large price tags, great horses can be found at reasonable prices.

On the other side of the coin are those ropers who spend too little on their horse compared to their other roping purchases. Do not place more value on looking the part with an expensive truck and trailer. Rather, invest more of your resources in a horse that will help you be successful.

When shopping, find a reliable horse seller with a good reputation. If visiting a professional horse trader, shop with one who has been in the business for years and can provide references from previous customers. Follow up the references to see how satisfied those customers are with their purchase.

While certain breeds of horses, such as the American Quarter Horse and American Paint Horse, dominate the team roping industry, one criterion that might not play as large a role as many might think is bloodline. While knowing the performance history of a horse's ancestors can be a good predictor of talents that lie within, some well-bred prospects may just lack the inner drive that it takes to win. Instead, focus more on the individual horse than his breeding.

Many riders starting out narrow the search by focusing on older, finished horses. This time-honored advice prevents beginners from trying to teach themselves and a horse the sport simultaneously—an inexperienced horse with an unskilled roper can be a dangerous combination. New ropers can find a good deal with an older horse: He is experienced but maybe costs less due to his age. Although an aged horse might not have a long career ahead of him, he can be great for the beginner and last until you are ready for something more advanced (fig. 4.3). However, it's important to be aware of lameness and other health issues that may accompany this wisdom. Before buying, make sure you have your veterinarian perform a pre-purchase exam.


## MANAGING MEDICAL ISSUES

While many team ropers don't automatically cross a prospect off the list because of health issues, such as those commonly found in older horses, that doesn't mean you should buy a horse without all the facts. A pre-purchase exam is a quick, usually simple way to expose some issues that could either "kill" the deal or provide important medical information to help you manage potential problems down the road.

During pre-purchase exams, a veterinarian typically performs a *flexion test*: He bends the horse's legs at the fetlock and knee for a specific amount of time and then watches the horse move. The prolonged bend followed by immediate movement often makes lameness visible. Then, the vet usually takes X-rays to catch hidden issues that could affect the horse's competitive career (fig. 4.4).

*Horses*

4.3 *Equine senior citizens can be gritty, talented competitors, as this 24-year-old gelding demonstrates.*

Good flexion is the key to solid team roping performance. Some horses, like many human athletes, perform quite well with a few minor aches. Chronic pain is something else and should be checked into further.

## Injury

Injury prevention, however, is just as important as diagnosing it after-the-fact. Dr. Britt Conklin, head of the Podiatry Unit at the well-known Reata Equine Hospital in Weatherford, Texas, and one of about a dozen equine podiatrists in the United States, said that he is concerned that many of today's amateur ropers are riding their horses only when competing and not physically training both sides of their horse's body equally.

Even though a typical roping run can last mere seconds, the pressure and stress placed on a horse's legs and other parts of his body during that period of time can be tremendous, particularly when he is subjected to multiple runs in a day. Dr. Dustin Dorris, a veterinarian at Conerstone Animal Hospital

4.4  *Pre-purchase exams are a smart idea for any prospect. Some horses, like many human athletes, perform quite well with a few minor aches. However, chronic pain is another matter, and should be checked into further.*

4.5 *Team roping horses, like any other athlete, can have sport-related injuries. For example, this heel horses' hard, sliding stops can eventually wear on his hind legs. This can lead to chronic pain if symptoms are left unchecked.*

in Stephenville, Texas, who also specializes in equine podiatry, agrees that although team roping horses don't work as long in a single performance as reiners, cutters, or even barrel horses, ropers should pay attention to proper preventative and other health care for career longevity.

However, prospective owners should not worry excessively about the pre-purchase exam's results for a previously injured horse. If the horse checks out sound in the pre-purchase exam—meaning he usually flexes well and trots cleanly on a hard surface—past injuries aren't going to be an issue for that horse. Remember, your horse could easily kick a trailer or another horse the day after an exam and have more problems result from that than from former health issues uncovered during the checkup.

Dr. Dorris says that while some injuries occur due to genetics, others are the result of the plain wear-and-tear of a performance athlete. He added that team roping has its own share of event-specific ailments, especially for horses' legs, and that ropers should be aware of them. For example, it is common for team roping horses to have problems show up in diagonally positioned limbs after a long career. More often than not, these issues crop up in the left front and right hind legs, because of the repetitive pattern they run.

Individual moves that make up a team roping run can cause specific injuries: Dr. Conklin says that when a *head horse* leaves the box to chase the steer, he is usually on the left lead, which can cause left-front leg strains and even breaks. As the horse begins to *rate* during the run, or find the position he needs to keep in relation to the steer after sprinting to catch up to it (see p. 117), he slows up and shifts his weight to the hind end before the drive to the left and facing up to the steer.

Another ailment that veterinarians see commonly in seasoned head horses is ringbone, which is a calcium buildup in joints of the lower limbs. This is caused by repetitive movements.

*Heel horses* have specific issues too, according to Drs. Conklin and Dorris. Heel horses may display hock and hind-end trouble, due to their hard stops (fig. 4.5). They also sprint fast to haze the steer at the beginning of the run, which can lead to front-leg issues.

In addition to leg ailments, team roping horses can develop a sore back. This may be due to anything from pulling a steer to painful hocks: Although a tender hock might seem like an unlikely cause of a back issue, a horse may compensate for a leg injury by assuming the workload in other parts of his body.

Back pain is often plain muscle soreness, but when the spine is the problem, many options are available. Injections, similar to those commonly used in the hocks, are helpful, as are anti-inflammatory drugs, chiropractic care, and acupuncture. Ropers should also not discount the value of simple rest.

4.6 *This horse displays the well-muscled hip, correct legs, and intelligent expression that indicates a well-rounded, athletic team roping horse.*

## Inherited Disease

Keep in mind, too, that breeding practices over the years have developed certain genetic defects that can shorten the lifespan of the horse or cause other health concerns. Among them are Hyperkalemic Periodic Paralysis (HYPP), which is a deadly genetic disease, and most often found in stock-breed bloodlines descending from the stallion Impressive, typically in either the Western pleasure or halter horse industries. It is a muscular disease caused by a hereditary genetic defect that leads to uncontrolled muscle twitching or profound muscle weakness, and in severe cases, may lead to collapse or death.

Another genetic disease to be aware of is Hereditary Equine Regional Dermal Asthenia (HERDA). It is linked to the stallion Poco Bueno, a foundation Quarter Horse. It affects tissue like the skin, causing lesions that fail to heal properly. The lesions are caused when external forces, such as when a horse is ridden under

*4.7 An expert opinion can help a novice decide if a horse is physically right for the job. Here, an experienced roper gives youth Tucker Elston advice about his recent run.*

saddle, which stresses the skin. This makes team roping impossible. A recessive disease, it makes only horses that inherit the defect from both parents symptomatic. A test is available to identify the non-symptomatic carriers.

Bear in mind, it is not only the Quarter Horse breed that is affected by inherited diseases such as these. Most stock horse breeds carry many of the same popular bloodlines. When possible, you should investigate any horse's genetic background carefully before purchase.

## BUILT FOR SUCCESS

Like any athlete, a team roping horse needs to have the proper build to do his job well (fig. 4.6). However, since the ideal horse doesn't exist, the experts have some guidelines about what imperfections you can live with and which are deal-breakers (fig. 4.7).

*Horses*

Many ropers believe that the best *head horses* are tall "mammoths" and that ideal *heel horses* are smaller and agile. However, both Rickey Green and Speed Williams advise that size is not so much a factor as is sound conformation and the heart to win.

Comprehensive, in-depth coverage of build is too vast for the scope of this book, but the tenets of what makes an equine athlete can be found in resources such as, *Conformation: The Relationship of Form to Function,* by Marvin Beeman, DVM, a former president of the American Association of Equine Practitioners. The booklet, published by the American Quarter Horse Association (1996), applies to almost any breed of horse, but particularly to those stock types most often used in team roping.

In *The American Quarter Horse* (The Lyons Press, 1998), author Steven D. Price says the well-conformed horse is more than the sum of his parts. He should give the overall impression of balanced symmetry, with all the parts coming together in pleasing proportion.

Price adds that when evaluating the horse, you should examine him from all sides, looking for straight legs and bone structure, blemishes that could indicate serious leg injuries, and good muscle structure in the hindquarters and through the shoulders.

Also, according to Green, in both head and heel horses, a sturdy horse weighing between 1,100 and 1,250 pounds will likely have the bulk capable of taking the jerk of cattle at the end of the rope.

## Legs and Feet

There are also other factors to consider with conformation. For example, when examining a horse's leg structure, Dr. Dorris advises to remember to look at hoof size in relation to the upper body: A horse with small hooves cannot support the bulk of his body.

A horse with straight pasterns, or too little angle in his pasterns, has another common problem. The angle between the lower joints is not great enough to disperse the concussion coming from the ground; instead of the lower leg taking the shock, it goes straight up the limb, which is harder on the horse overall. "Upright" horses may see more arthritic injuries down the road.

On the other hand, horses with too much angle in the pastern could see more soft tissue setbacks, because structures like the suspensory ligaments are taking on some of the concussion that would be dealt with by bone in a properly conformed leg.

Determining the proper angle for your individual horse depends on that horse's overall conformation: The angle of the *front leg* fetlock down to the hoof should match the angle of the shoulder blade from the spine to the point of the shoulder. And, with the *hind leg*, Speed Williams has had great success with horses that have a short pastern, low hocks, and a leg that is not

4.8 *This horse, owned and led by Rickey Green, demonstrates the physical qualities professionals look for in team roping.*

too straight. The hind leg should angle under the horse a bit from the hocks down, so the horse can tuck his hindquarters under and balance during the sharp movements called for in team roping.

## Neck and Headset

Rickey Green adds that how the head and neck ties into the body of the horse is also a factor in a roping horse. This is not just for fluidity of movement, but also because if your horse's head and neck is physically in the way of your swing or throw, you must maneuver around it to catch a steer. So, a low headset is preferred by most ropers, with the neck coming straight from the withers for heel horses and slightly higher for head horses (fig. 4.8).

*Horses*

*4.9 While what is on the inside is most important when choosing a horse, his color and markings may be also be a factor when you are making your selection. Be aware that white-faced beauties, like this palomino overo, could be a bit more susceptible to sunburn in areas with hot, sunny summers. And, grey horses are susceptible to melanomas, a type of skin cancer.*

The horse should be able to tuck his nose toward his chest and pick his head up higher than the withers when cued with the reins. Doing so helps him place his weight on his hind end to handle the impact of the steer better.

A shorter-necked heel horse will let a heeler stay in closer to the steer, yet still see its hind feet as he rounds the corner. However, a neck that is too short doesn't provide the flexibility in the poll that allows a horse to tuck in his nose. It also positions the neck too close to the saddle horn when the nose is tucked, which makes it more difficult to dally.

## COLOR AND MARKINGS

Color and markings can also make a difference in your choice of horse. Gray horses may need extra attention to guard against melanoma, a type of skin cancer. Spotted horses—especially those that have white markings with underlying pink skin—may need protection from sunburn (fig. 4.9). These horses may also have striped or white hooves, which can be softer and require more care.

4.10 *In summary, physical durability and good training are the most important attributes of a great team roping horse. Solid equine citizens—like this horse, one of Rickey Green's—are worth every penny because of their longevity and dependability.*

Whatever physical type of horse you choose, the experts agree that you should select for solid training and physical durability over good looks (or color) and a fancy pedigree, especially if you are a first-time team roper. Confidence-building horses, even plain ones, are always in demand and will help a new roper advance more quickly (fig. 4.10).

*Horses*

Building a
Foundation

# ROPER GROUNDWORK

**L**IKE EVERY STURDY STRUCTURE, education begins with a strong foundation. Learning how to become a team roper is no exception. With this sport, you literally build your skills from the ground up. Beginners first practice while standing on their own two feet and must earn their way onto a horse's back.

## GETTING STARTED

After studying the basics of team roping and gaining a general understanding of the sport, it is time to test the waters with hands-on practice. But, before you can try to rope anything, you first need to learn how to hold and swing a rope. (It may help you to refer back to chapter 2—p. 31—where I discuss the rope and the function of each part.)

First, you need to know where to hold the all-important *loop* (fig. 5.1). To locate the proper place to hold the *spoke*, you must consider the entire loop. Generally, with an outstretched arm, the *eye* should be halfway between your hand, which is at the loop's highest point, and the *tip*, which is the point of the loop closest to the ground.

Next, ropers must learn the proper way to grip with their hand, which leads to more efficient swings and throws:

1   If you are right-handed, lay the two strands of the rope in the palm of your hand with the top strand to the right (see fig. 2.3 D, p. 34).

2   Extend your index finger and place it under the top strand, then place your thumb on top of both strands. When the top strand is on the left side of the bottom strand, you have less control of the loop during the swing and throw.

3   Rather than holding the spoke in your palm, grip it in your fingers during the swing, and stabilize it with your index finger and thumb.

Although it isn't actually a part held by the roper, the portion of rope between your two hands is also important. To gauge the proper distance between the hand holding the loop and the one gripping the *coils*, hold the coils to the middle of your chest. Then, stretch your other hand out straight out from your side. The length of rope between your two hands should be the proper length to get you started. Any extra length gets in the way of reining and dallying, while too little can impede the swing and throw (fig. 5.2).

Coils are held in the rein hand. One or more coils may be "dropped" as needed to rope a faraway steer or to enlarge your loop. Ideally, these circles of extra rope should grow progressively smaller as they get closer to the loop. This prevents them from tangling with each other or your hand when you drop one.

While the actual diameter of the coils can be adjusted to what feels right to each individual, novices should take care to not make them too small or too big. Either extreme can be dangerous. When wrapped too closely around the hand, a missed dally or loss of control over the rope could leave you with trapped or damaged fingers. However, coils should not be sized so large that they are in the way when reining or dallying.

## Swing Right

After a new roper masters how to hold a rope properly, it is then time to master the basic swing. This motion keeps the loop wide open while it is pivoting through the air around your head (fig. 5.3).

A lot of beginning ropers are confused as to how a loop should feel when in motion. Many are given the vague instruction that swinging a rope is "all in the wrist." Rickey Green instead suggests swinging the rope the way you would swing a bucket of water around your head (fig. 5.4). You want to feel weight on the loop as it moves around, just like you would if you were trying to keep the water from sloshing out of the bucket.

5.1 *The first step to becoming a team roper is learning how to hold the loop. Proper hand placement is shown here. Note that the eye is about halfway between the hand and the loop's tip (the point closest to the ground).*

5.2 *Craig Bray demonstrates how to measure the proper distance between the hands when holding a rope. Ideally, when the coils are held to the chest, there should be an arm's length of rope extending to the hand holding the loop.*

5.3 *Rickey Green instructs his daughter, Whitney, on proper swing technique. The swing keeps the loop open while it pivots around the head in preparation for the throw.*

5.4 *Another student of Green, Zeb Allen, practices his swing. Green advises visualizing swinging a bucket of water around your head. You want to feel weight on the loop as it moves around, just like you would if you were trying to keep the water from sloshing out of the bucket.*

To "feel" the tip of the rope (or the imaginary bucket), Green suggests envisioning the path of your swing as following the course of the hands on a clock. This allows a roper to use centrifugal force correctly. With practice, you should be able to "feel" the tip of the rope as it passes each quarter-hour mark on your clock while swinging your rope around your head.

One of the most important lessons is how to turn the rope over during the swing's rotation, so that the bottom strand flips to the top as the rope comes around your head during the swing (fig. 5.5). Learning this step properly takes "feel," which only comes, again, with practice. Most experts agree that you should turn your hand and the rope over between three o'clock, which is at shoulder level, and two o'clock, which is about even with your ear, as you

*5.5 Rickey Green instructs student Zeb Allen in the art of turning over his loop during the swing's rotation, so that the bottom strand flips to the top as the rope comes around his head during the swing. Learning this step properly takes "feel," which only comes with practice.*

swing your rope counterclockwise. Raising your elbow above your hand as your hand is turning over is one aid that may help you accomplish this goal.

Once you are able to hold a rope and begin to swing, you can begin to learn how to feed additional rope through the eye to increase the size of your loop. Done incorrectly, however, the loop can twist, making it ineffective. The shape it commonly curls into looks like the number eight, so when the loop does this, it is called "figure-eighting."

Many new ropers sidestep this issue for a while by starting out with a large loop, rather than feeding it to the final size. They learn to feed the rope later on, when they are more confident with holding and swinging a loop. Most ropers learn the technique by simple trial and error.

## Throwing the Rope

For a proper delivery of the loop, Green says to think again of a clock when you are learning to throw (fig. 5.6). A good rule of thumb with throwing is to point your fingertips in the direction slightly to the left of the target—at about eleven o'clock if the target is twelve o'clock. This is different than the traditional school of thought, which said that a roper should point directly at target.

Green adds that your index finger must stay inside the center of the loop when throwing. Point it too much, and the loop actually becomes narrower. This makes a catch harder to accomplish. The index finger can be open, and create a wider base for your swing, but pressure must be applied to the rope between the thumb and index finger.

When throwing, remember to aim all your fingertips, instead of just the index finger. However, the actual method is different, depending on whether you are a *header* or *heeler*. Not only does the angle of swing change for each role, so does the angle of launch.

5.6 *Green advises his students envision following the path of a clock's hands when learning to throw. Ideally, they point their fingertips to eleven o'clock, or just to the left of the target, as shown here.*

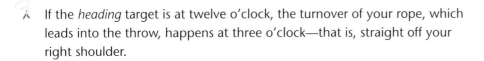 If the *heading* target is at twelve o'clock, the turnover of your rope, which leads into the throw, happens at three o'clock—that is, straight off your right shoulder.

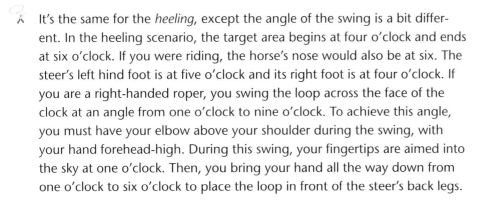 It's the same for the *heeling*, except the angle of the swing is a bit different. In the heeling scenario, the target area begins at four o'clock and ends at six o'clock. If you were riding, the horse's nose would also be at six. The steer's left hind foot is at five o'clock and its right foot is at four o'clock. If you are a right-handed roper, you swing the loop across the face of the clock at an angle from one o'clock to nine o'clock. To achieve this angle, you must have your elbow above your shoulder during the swing, with your hand forehead-high. During this swing, your fingertips are aimed into the sky at one o'clock. Then, you bring your hand all the way down from one o'clock to six o'clock to place the loop in front of the steer's back legs.

Using the idea of swinging an imaginary bucket of water over your head as your guide, you should allow the weight of the water to carry your bucket (the tip of your loop) to the dummy. Do not use the force of your hand. Ropers should follow through with their throw by bringing their fingertips around the circle of the clock face toward the target. This action creates the needed power to launch the loop (fig. 5.7).

5.7 *Using the idea of swinging an imaginary bucket of water over your head as your guide, for maximum power you should allow the weight of the water to carry your bucket (the tip of your loop) to the dummy, not the force of your hand. Here, Green demonstrates proper technique.*

## CATCHING THE DUMMY

After a student masters holding, swinging, and throwing a rope, the next step is to work on the ground with a stationary dummy to learn how to catch (fig. 5.8). Much can be learned about necessary catching technique using a stationary dummy.

Rickey Green and Speed Williams use the same procedures to teach students to catch, whether they are there for a single lesson or long-term coaching. How fast you advance depends quite a bit on your dedication to practice, but the benefit of a roping dummy is it is always ready when you are. Catching the dummy should be the primary skill learned at this point, as holding and throwing the rope can be practiced without a target.

Although there are several ways to teach a header to catch the horns, Williams recommends focusing on catching the right horn first, and then laying your loop over the left horn. This technique is not as complicated to learn as some other methods, and a roper doesn't have to be placed in a perfect position to make a good catch.

Positioning is also very important in your practice. Ideally, the *header* should stand to the left of the dummy, about 3 to 4 feet away. Pretend you are on horseback to gauge how far back to stand. You should be about the length of a horse's neck behind the dummy's tail—as if the horse's nose is even with the dummy's hindquarters. The *heeler* should be only slightly to the left of the dummy's hind legs and, again, a horse's neck-length back, as if the horse's nose is just to the left and slightly ahead of the dummy's tail.

Work on getting very consistent catching at these basic positions before you try more difficult ones. Ultimately, you want to practice in various positions because there will be times in the arena when you have to take shots from less-than-ideal locations.

Green steps up the challenge for his students by placing a large, round trash can lid over the dummy's horns and asking them to rope the dummy without knocking off the lid (fig. 5.9). Eventually, Williams has his students begin swinging the rope

5.8 *After learning to swing and throw, the next step is to learn how to catch. Like the previous steps, practice makes perfect with catching. Here, Green gauges his daughter's technique.*

5.9  *One drill Green uses to reinforce his students' focus and technique is to have them throw their loop around a trash can lid placed on the dummy's horns. The goal is to make the catch without knocking off the lid. Once mastered, students often find it easier to throw at and catch more realistic targets later.*

5.10  *Eventually, Speed Williams has his students ramp up the level of difficulty by learning to walk into position before throwing. This heeler got creative when stepping up the challenge by swinging at a live steer.*

while walking up to the dummy (or even a live steer), and throwing once they are in the correct position (fig. 5.10). This helps simulate real action, where ropers have to ride up to the steer and find the proper position before they can have a reliable chance of catching.

## Choosing a Practice Dummy

As mentioned in chapter 2 (p. 41), practice dummies may be made from an assortment of materials. They range from very basic designs to ones with "bells and whistles." *Heelers* can start out with something as rudimentary as a sawhorse (fig. 5.11). *Headers* can begin with a set of rawhide-covered horns in

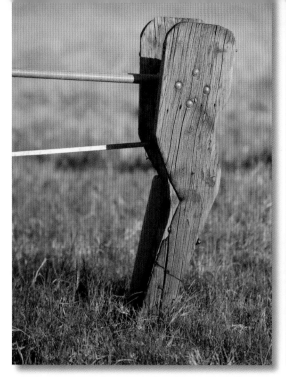

5.11 *Dummies don't need to be fancy or expensive. This basic wooden one serves heelers just as well as a more elaborate version.*

5.12 *Even professionals do just fine with rudimentary practice dummies. This is Rickey Green's personal heading dummy. It was made for him by his uncle, champion team roper Walt Woodard. It consists of a basic metal frame covered with carpet and a horn wrap.*

a bale of hay or mounted on a pipe frame. Even experts have proven to do just fine with homemade devices. For a heading dummy, Green uses a pipe frame covered in carpet, with a horn wrap—the head protection that live cattle wear during competition—around the horns (fig. 5.12).

Several types of quality, manufactured dummies are available if you don't have the time, inclination, or skills to build your own. They are readily available at tack stores that sell team roping gear. Beware, however, of purchasing one made from smooth materials, like plastic. Without a horn wrap to add grip, plastic dummies can allow your rope to slip.

Whatever type of dummy you choose, it is important to our two experts that this be your first learning tool. Not only does practice on the ground make learning team roping safer, it gives you a leg up when you are ready to learn advanced techniques as you won't have taught yourself bad habits that must be undone. Bad muscle memory can be deadly for a team roper's technique, and bad habits can kill your run, warns Williams.

## Dummy Roping Competition

If you are a team roper 12 years or under, you are in luck—there is a special dummy roping competition just for you (fig. 5.13). Show off your skills through USTRC's Junior Looper Program, which awards talent for catching the horns of a stationary dummy. These youth competitions are always held during a *sanctioned* event, and you can go home with prestigious titles and great prizes like buckles and trophy saddles.

There are three age divisions for USTRC Junior Loopers: six and under, seven to nine, and 10 to 12. The competition season for each runs from November 1 of one year to October 1 of the next. While entry is free, children must present either their current USTRC membership card or a valid birth certificate the day of an event in order to participate.

The basic format of each division's event asks contestants to take turns roping. Those who make a single, legal catch with one loop advance to the next round. After each round, remaining entries move progressively farther away from the target, which increases the level of difficulty. When a final roper is left, prizes and titles are awarded.

## Safety and Children

Many professional instructors, like Speed Williams, are adamant about the safety of children, providing them with sound information and advice in addition to a competition just for them. At his website, www. speedroping.com, most videos are subscriber-based—with the notable exceptions being any that pertain to children, which are free to watch. Parents can go there to learn more about teaching their children safe, reliable techniques.

5.13 *Children 12 years of age and younger are invited to participate in USTRC dummy roping competitions, such as the one seen here. Entry is free, and winners can take home prestigious titles and great prizes, like trophy saddles and championship buckles.*

## LEARN FASTER WITH A TEACHER

The tips offered by the experts in this book are fairly general. While they will get you started on the right track, questions are bound to crop up. That is where a more experienced team roper can help. Even experienced professionals like Green and Williams say that they continue to learn from other experienced ropers throughout their career—no matter how advanced they are—and that ropers should always strive to improve.

Finding the right teacher can make any learning curve much easier to navigate (fig. 5.14). As a novice, you should seriously consider finding a more experienced team roper to help you learn instead of going it alone. For many, the hunt for a teacher can be relatively easy. Some lucky ropers don't have to

look any further for a knowledgeable team roper to help them learn than a friendly next-door neighbor. Others have to look a little harder.

Flip through the latest issue of the USTRC's *SuperLooper Magazine,* or do a quick Web search, and you are sure to find plenty of experienced professional instructors from across the nation advertising their services—hopefully some very near where you live.

Or, attend a roping event in your area—not to compete, but to introduce yourself as a beginning roper and ask about local instructors and arenas where you can go to practice. Newcomers should not be afraid to speak to better ropers. Both Williams and Green credit several seasoned competitors for their growth in the sport and attribute their success directly to the other team ropers' kindness and their individual courage to ask for the help.

You will find ads for ropings all over the country both in *SuperLooper* and on the USTRC's website (www.ustrc.com). In addition, instructors often offer public educational opportunities, which can be a great place to meet other area team ropers and to learn about your local team roping community.

If you are considering attending one of the team roping schools that many professionals produce, certain skills must already be mastered to maximize your time. For beginners, a better option might be a seminar or another opportunity that isn't as hands-on. (To learn more about team roping schools, and to see if you are ready to attend one, read Rickey Green's checklist in the next chapter—p. 97.)

5.14 *New ropers can learn faster at all levels with an instructor. Here, Rickey Green holds a lesson on technique with daughter Whitney and student Zeb Allen.*

## GETTING STARTED WITHOUT AN INSTRUCTOR

If a personal mentor isn't available to you, don't despair. Beginners still have many options available to them—much more so than when the sport first began—and you can get a good roping foundation on your own. With the rapid expansion of the Internet, and its wide selection of videos and other learning material, the average roper today comes to the sport far more educated than his predecessors.

Three options are available for you to gain knowledge if you don't have the benefit of your own personal team roping instructor. Each has its place, and a combination of each, along with practice, may be the most effective way for you to learn until you can find someone to gauge your form and show you the rest.

## Live Speakers

Listen to professional team roping speakers live when available to you (fig. 5.15). The major benefit of this type of communication is your immediate ability to interact with an expert and ask specific questions tailored to your situation. Examples include everything from quick, public seminars to detailed week-long schools. The cost of such opportunities can be anywhere from zero to a few hundred dollars.

Although you might not be ready to participate hands-on, many team roping schools will let you attend as a "non-enrolled audience member." As an added benefit, this is often at a reduced fee, or sometimes at no cost at all—especially if you are accompanying someone who is an enrolled student.

## Videos

The next "get-started" educational option is video: A set of training DVDs produced by experts; television shows; and, of course, all the programs you can find for viewing on the Internet, are an easy way to quickly gain knowledge from the comfort of your own home, and you can watch them repeatedly.

Entire television cable networks have been created in the past couple of decades that cater to the horse market. Many professionals from all equine disciplines have introduced themselves to new audiences through these cable shows, and team roping is no exception. Check your provider's listings for available programs.

In addition, the current popularity of video as an effective communications tool has multiplied with the rise of the Internet. Personal websites, like Rickey Green's www.powerteamroping.com, and public sites, like YouTube, have made films far more cost-effective to distribute. Others, like Speed Williams' www.speedroping.com have also embraced cutting-edge social media to alert visitors about fresh videos as they become available.

However you view a video, be aware that while it offers much of the same information as a live speaker, it does come with its own set of limitations. For example, films tend to provide more "generic" information and content not tailored to individuals.

5.15 *Novices can learn a lot by simply listening to more experienced team ropers as they lecture or teach others. Here, Zeb Allen observes while Rickey Green explains a tip about catching a dummy to another student.*

## Reading Material

You should not forget to also include printed materials in your educational arsenal. Examples include books, magazines, and websites that are text-and-photo-based. While seeing a live speaker and watching videos are great tools that show action, you can miss out on the ability to review and study a lesson in depth. Finally, Green says that many people simply retain knowledge more readily when looking at still photos and inked text.

## YOU MUST EARN TALENT

A new team roper will get out of the sport exactly what he is prepared to put into it. If you work extremely long hours or spend the majority of your leisure time on other activities, you can't expect to progress as quickly as the teenager who practices six hours a day all summer. Keep this in mind when you are setting your team roping goals.

However you learn about team roping, when you have mastered the exercises in this chapter and can rope your dummy consistently, our experts say you are prepared to continue.

But, before you are ready to progress to roping from horseback, you must be able to ride with confidence and be able to swing, throw, and catch with skill. In chapter 6 we will explore the prerequisites Green and Williams require before allowing students to attempt team roping from the saddle. Plus, pick up some tips from top horsemanship expert Clinton Anderson.

# 6

# GOOD HORSEMANSHIP SKILLS

**B**EFORE ANY GOOD TEACHER puts a rope in your hand, Rickey Green and Speed Williams agree that you should test your horsemanship. At this point, it's not about roping, but how to balance atop a moving horse.

If you have not yet mastered basic riding skills, there is no sense trying to rope (fig. 6.1). Attempting this sport before you have a handle on your seat and your horse increases the risk of things going wrong, potentially leading to dangerous consequences.

When Williams initially evaluates a new student, he sees how well the student maintains proper form when following a mechanical steer at a trot (fig. 6.2). He maintains that beginners must pass this first test before going forward with anything else on horseback.

Learning how to correctly post a trot, which is required in Williams' test, trains you to rely on your legs—not the reins—for balance when you are up out of the saddle. Since team ropers spend much of their run leaning forward, balanced in their stirrups and hovering over the seat of the saddle, it is a very

6.1 *Horsemanship is key to transitioning to roping from the saddle. If you aren't a proficient rider, there is no reason to try something with as many different elements as roping cattle from horseback. Our experts strongly advise you confirm basic riding skills first.*

6.2 *Speed Williams first tests a student's riding ability by having the student trot behind a mechanical steer with a pretend rope. Rickey Green also teaches his students this basic step.*

important lesson. You need to realize that team roping's forward posture is different than that used in many other Western events, where the rider sits further back and plants his weight in the saddle's seat.

The hardest thing about team roping is the riding, says Green, who cautions that those who have not learned to ride well first will often take much longer to teach the skills of the sport. Responsible teachers will provide inexperienced riders practice drills to brush up on essential riding skills, and many team roping experts offer videos and other learning material dedicated to good horsemanship.

# RIDER PRE-FLIGHT CHECKLIST

To test if you are ready to move on to mounted roping, Rickey Green provides a quick checklist of requirements. Mastering the first two doesn't just mean that you have performed them once before and might be able to duplicate the results again; it means that you are able do them every time, anytime, and anywhere. The third is the all-important rule-of-thumb for all beginner ropers.

1  *You should be able to comfortably ride the walk, trot, and lope with a stable seat* (fig. 6.3). Roping is a high-speed event, and a rider should be confident sprinting down an arena after a steer. However, all three gaits may be needed during the course of a competition or practice day. Remember too, that team roping isn't a sport of straight lines and smooth transitions between gallops and halts. The twists, turns, and sudden accelerations and decelerations can be challenging to sit. Green strongly advises riders to be able to handle abrupt changes before they decide to complicate things with a rope.

2  *You need the ability to rate the pace of your horse.* This means that before you charge down an arena at top speed, you need to know that you can slow and stop your horse on command. Or, if you draw a steer that seems to sprout wings, you should be able to ask for more speed from your horse to catch up to it. (Learn more about *rate* on p. 117.)

3  *A green rider should never be matched with an inexperienced horse.* Have a horse that has done the job before. Do not plan on training your horse to team rope while you are still learning yourself. (For more tips on finding the right heading or heeling horse, refer to chapter 4, p. 67.)

*6.3 Enthusiasts should have a stable seat at all gaits before they complicate things with a rope. Here, Paul Melvin rides with ease as he lopes his horse in a warm-up.*

6.4 A–C *A gelding tied with too long a lead rope (A), too short a lead rope, and one of an appropriate length (C). The correct length allows him to maintain his natural headset.*

## BASIC GROUND HANDLING

### Secure Tying

Not all good horsemanship happens in the saddle. Although ropers tend to be smart about competition equipment, even experienced ones are sometimes less informed about tack used outside the arena, particularly halters and lead ropes. It is as important to make safety a priority when you are on foot as when you are mounted.

One problem seen all-to-often at team roping events is when multiple horses are tied to temporary panels or secured to other unsafe fencing. A closely related issue is that many horses are simply tied improperly. This can take many forms, including the length of lead between the horse and what he is tied to. Owners who leave their horse *tied with extra length* in the lead often think they are doing their horse a kindness by giving him the opportunity to nibble from the ground (fig. 6.4 A). However, a horse can easily entangle a leg or wrap the rope around a nearby object, and if he panics, there can be serious consequences—from rope burns to far more severe injuries.

On the other hand, when a horse is *tied too closely*, it can force him to keep his head unnaturally high (fig. 6.4 B). After a while, this can tire a horse and cause soreness that will affect the way he performs.

For safety, your horse should be tied fairly short above withers-height, at a distance that allows his head and neck to maintain a neutral position (fig. 6.4 C). Also, be sure to use some sort of quick-release knot, which is easily undone in case of emergency. Entire books have been written about knots alone, so I won't specifically cover them here.

## Haltering

Another common error involves haltering. Rope halters popular today have many benefits, but owners must be educated about how to use them. For example, many users are unaware of the proper way to tie the knot that holds this type of halter in place.

When tied correctly, the end coming over the horse's poll should slip behind and through the loop attached at the top of the left cheek piece. Next, it should be wrapped around to the right, then behind the loop. This forms a second loose loop when the end is circled back around the left side of the loop to the front.

At that point, the tail should then be tucked from near the horse's eye through the newly formed loop, down toward the jaw, and pulled snug (fig. 6.5 A). Many times people do this backward, leaving the tail flapping near the horse's eye (fig. 6.5 B). When the tail is too long, it can actually rub into the horse's eye. This is not only annoying, but can be dangerous with a head-shy or nervous horse.

*Good Horsemanship Skills*

6.5 A & B *Rope halters have become very popular. They need to be properly fitted snugly against the horse's head. Also, the securing knot must be tied correctly, with the tail directed away from the horse's eye (A), rather than backward, allowing the knot to rub near the horse's sensitive eye (B).*

## THE FIVE BODY PARTS: DRILLS TO TEST SOFTNESS AND FLEXIBILITY

If some of your horsemanship skills could use polishing, that's okay. Green advises novices to allow at least a year to learn to become a confident rider before attempting team roping from horseback. During the meantime, consider riding lessons, learn about proper roping technique, and build a solid foundation with the groundwork covered in the previous chapter.

Clinton Anderson, a well-known clinician and horsemanship expert, also suggests using this time to tune-up your horse's technique. You can learn more about him and his horsemanship tips at www.downunderhorsemanship. com. He also has authored several books on the subject, including *Clinton Anderson's Downunder Horsemanship: Establishing Respect and Control for English and Western Riders* and *Clinton Anderson's Lessons Well Learned: Why My Method Works for Any Horse* (Trafalgar Square Books, www.horseandriderbooks.com).

Regardless of the sport, he first recommends an easy set of five drills for your equine athlete. Each one tests the softness and flexibility of the horse's five major body parts: the head and neck; poll; shoulders; rib cage; and hindquarters. This series ensures that your horse is listening to you, and increases your odds of a quick response when you need it, which could be very important someday as you are flying down the arena after a steer.

Anderson has a quick test to see if your horse is a bit rusty and could use a refresher course in "respect." Simply ride your horse in a halter and lead rope instead of a bridle and tie-down (fig. 6.6). If your horse is pushy and resistant, chances are he needs a a tune-up.

Your horse's mouth is nothing but a telegraph station, and Anderson says that any stiffness present in the horse's body comes through to his mouth. He adds that when you get everything behind the mouth "soft and supple," the mouth will feel like velvet. Speed Williams agrees that a "soft" horse makes the best partner (fig. 6.7). So, when trying a prospect out for the first time, he suggests you ask him to flex his head and neck, and bend his body.

Although you eventually want the horse's body to work in unison to do the job you give it, the quickest way to do so is to train each of the five body parts separately. Once you have control of all five, you will find you have better command of the entire horse.

6.6 *Clinton Anderson has a quick test to see if your horse is a bit rusty and could use a refresher course in horsemanship drills. Simply ride your horse in a halter and lead rope instead of a bridle and tie-down, as the rider is doing here. If your horse is pushy and resistant, chances are he needs a tune-up.*

6.7 *Speed Williams says that a "soft" horse makes the best partner. Here, novice roper Zeb Allen's horse demonstrates that mental attitude with a willing, quiet stop.*

6.8 *Between a horse and rider, the horse will always come out ahead in a physical contest because he's stronger. So, Anderson says the weaker human must out-think the horse to win. This is where leverage helps, in the form of his lateral flexion exercise.*

6.9 *Later, when the horse is light and responsive to the lateral flexion cue, you can try to establish vertical flexion and may find the horse obeys you without resistance. For the best results, practice both drills often.*

## Head, Neck, and Poll

What if you have a high-headed, stiff horse? In order to get a horse to drop his head and tuck his nose easily, called *vertical flexion*, you must teach him Anderson's first drill—how to bend his head and neck around laterally (fig. 6.8). The goal is to just get the horse to "give" to the pressure when you signal with the reins—in any direction.

Between a horse and rider, the horse will always come out ahead in a physical contest because he's stronger. So, the weaker human must out-think the horse to win. This is where leverage helps. Instead of pulling straight back on the reins, use lateral flexion—that is, take up one rein to direct the horse's nose toward the stirrup on the same side. One rein pulls the horse off balance and gives you an advantage.

Later, when the horse is light and responsive to the cue for lateral flexion, you can try to establish vertical flexion and may find the horse obeys you without resistance (fig. 6.9). However, even if your horse is great the first time you ask for either response, regularly practice both lateral and vertical flexion for continuing best results.

## Shoulders

Next, Anderson says to work the "steering wheel" of the horse—his shoulders. However, make sure you're prepared to move your horse to this step by testing his willingness to move at the gait you choose, and that he stops when asked.

Start this two-part drill by having the horse move his shoulders off leg pressure by going forward at a 45-degree angle (fig. 6.10). After the horse has mastered this technique, ramp it up with *counterbending*. This is the same movement, except the horse's nose is tipped *away* from the direction the horse's shoulders are going. Counterbending should be practiced in both directions, and eventually, at all three gaits.

## Rib Cage

To gain control of the horse's rib cage, Anderson says that circles are your best friend. To begin, walk the horse in a small circle, 3 to 4 feet in diameter (fig. 6.11). By taking the slack out of your inside rein, your horse's head and neck should softly bend around the imaginary line you are traveling—especially if you have practiced lateral flexion. His ribs should follow suit and continue the curve through his entire body. If not, you can encourage this by bumping him with your inside calf. Ultimately, you want the horse to hold this frame even on a loose rein.

6.10 *Next, focus on the "steering wheel" of your horse—his shoulders. Start this by having the horse move his shoulders off leg pressure by going forward at a 45-degree angle. Here, the horse is doing just that. Notice his front legs crossing as he steps sideways as well as forward.*

6.11 *Arching your horse's body as he moves around a small circle brings you control of the horse's rib cage—another element in Clinton Anderson's path to horsemanship success. Ultimately, you want your horse to maintain his good form while on a loose rein, like this gelding is demonstrating.*

## Hindquarters

The last of the body parts to master are the hindquarters, which Anderson calls the horse's "engine." Your horse's ability to go faster, stop, and turn all comes from the hindquarters. As it is one of the main components in getting a horse to collect and soften to the bit, the sooner you can get control of the hindquarters, the better.

A foundation exercise Anderson uses for a horse's hips is "disengaging" the hindquarters. Begin by standing still when mounted. Reach back with one leg and cue the horse to step one hind foot across the other to the side. The point of this exercise is to reinforce to the horse that you are in control of his powerful engine when you are astride. As an additional aid to help the horse understand, tip the horse's nose away from the direction you are asking the hips to move (fig. 6.12).

You can later advance this drill by putting the horse in motion, then asking him in yield his hindquarters to a stop. Eventually, the horse should progress to performing the exercise at all three gaits.

Seasoned horses can have a tendency to be independent thinkers and take control. Each of Anderson's drills reminds the horse to wait for instructions from you and reinforces that you are the leader in your riding partnership. For best results, give your horse instant release from rein or leg pressure when he performs these drills correctly.

## AWAY FROM THE PRACTICE PEN

While it is important to spend quality time with your horse inside the arena, what you do outside of the arena is also a part of good horsemanship, and may be just as significant to your equine partner. While practice is important, if your horse only associates you with endless drills, he can sour on the prospect of being with you.

To balance this, Rickey Green suggests that about half the time you spend with your horse, do low-key activities your horse can appreciate, like taking him out of the stall to be hand grazed in lush grass, or go for an easy trail ride. This part of your training encourages him to enjoy just being around you.

This need for downtime doesn't mean that a team roping horse doesn't like his job. Most roping horses are stock horses, bred to handle cows and perform other duties on a ranch. Their love for the work is often as much a part of their genetic makeup as coat color or height. Many of the injuries seen in heading and heeling horses are actually caused by these equine athletes pushing their body too far in order to get the job done.

## GET READY TO ROPE

When you're ready, an expert can put you on the fast track to proficiency, but your greatest concern is to find someone who is reputable. While professional help is great, do not discount the benefits of knowing an experienced non-pro team roper. Often a low- or no-cost option, they are often easy to find at your nearest practice arena. As mentioned in the last chapter, whether you are on the hunt for someone to give you quick advice or to answer your questions in-depth, the places where ropers gather can be a great resource. There, you can find knowledgeable amateur team ropers with tips about how to perfect your horsemanship, and later, how to rope from the saddle.

Once you have confidence in your ability to rope from the ground and ride and handle your horse, it is time to put those skills together. Turn the page to take the next step.

6.12 *Anderson suggests "disengaging" the hindquarters for "engine" control. This foundation exercise asks the horse to cross his hind feet over as he steps sideways away from your leg cue. This rider is helping her gelding learn the move by tipping his nose in the opposite direction from where she is asking the horse's hips to go.*

*Good Horsemanship Skills*

# 7

# ROPING FROM HORSEBACK

NOW THAT YOU'VE LAID A GOOD FOUNDATION, you are ready to become a team roper in the classic sense. You should by now have an idea if you want to be a *header* or a *heeler*, or if, perhaps, you want to become an all-around team roper who does it all. Whatever your goals, this chapter contains both general and specific tips to help get you started roping from horseback.

## PRACTICE STILL MAKES PERFECT

Set yourself up for success before entering a competition. This means practicing anything new well in advance of the big day. In short, be prepared to handle whatever situation unpredictable cattle might throw at you.

The first step for any novice who wants to learn to rope live cattle is to find a place to practice that has knowledgeable ropers who don't mind helping

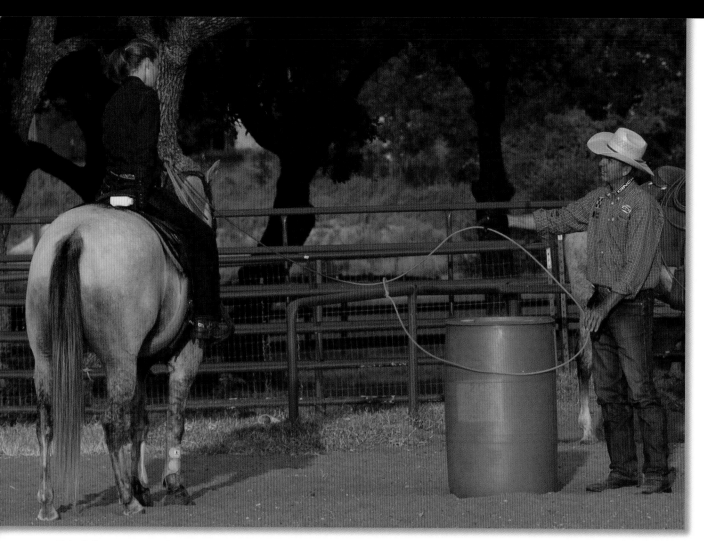

7.1 *Other ropers can be a great source of knowledge about the sport, especially once you move to mounted work. Here, Rickey Green tells a rider to envision her loop making a circle wide enough to catch a barrel when she throws.*

you learn (fig. 7.1). Professional or amateur ropers can play just as big of a role now, when you are learning to rope from horseback, as they did earlier in the learning process.

If you live in an area where roping is popular, you are in luck. Often, local public or private arenas hold weekly practices where ropers of all levels can learn, usually at very affordable prices. To find one, search online and visit businesses that cater to ropers, such as local feed and tack stores.

Word of mouth can be your best bet when hunting for other team ropers. Don't discount the importance of the local coffee shop, which can be a major communication hub—especially in rural areas. Be social. Visit with the "regulars" as they often know the comings and goings around town. Even if someone doesn't personally team rope, he may know an instructor or an arena that holds practices.

If you decide to visit a public practice session, call ahead and ask if they rope a mechanical steer or live cattle. Be sure also to inquire about the number of people that usually attend: A small, controlled practice with fewer people and a mechanical dummy is often better until you're more comfortable with the different aspects of the sport. It can be daunting to jump right into dealing with unpredictable live cattle.

If you live in an area far from other team ropers, you are still not out of options to progress with your training. Rickey Green suggests that you try borrowing, renting, or buying a mechanical steer to get started, especially when you are training on your own (see below). Once you are able to rope the machine proficiently, enroll in a team roping school where you can learn to rope live cattle. Then, you can attend some competitions, make acquaintances, and eventually practice with them.

*7.2 A mechanical steer is an important step that makes the transition between a stationary dummy and live cattle easier. It is especially important if you are training without other team ropers.*

## Mechanical Steer

Both Green and Williams suggest a mechanical steer for learning all mounted work (fig. 7.2). However, if you only have access to live steers, you should follow the same methods outlined on the pages that follow to become familiar with working cattle. Just be aware that your road will be harder.

Mechanical steers come with several advantages for a new roper, especially those training on their own. The largest benefit is that you don't need an arena to use one. Any open area will do. Also, while many ropers are reluctant to pay the cost of a mechanical steer, it might be the wisest, most economical investment you can make.

Another top advantage of mechanical steers is the sheer number of runs you can make—the machines don't need rest, like real steers, and will go as long as you can. Also, unlike live steers, a machine can make the same run at the same intensity as long as a roper needs it to. Varying moods and personalities do not come into play, unlike real cattle, which come equipped with different temperaments and athletic capabilities. Both make it tougher for a novice to practice a tricky scenario repeatedly until he's mastered it.

## Tracking

However you get started, your first step to roping from horseback is *tracking*, which means finding and maintaining the proper position for you and your horse in relation to the steer. Once you are satisfied that you have a solid foundation in riding and can catch a dummy from the ground, tracking is considered the final test before roping from the box.

7.3 *Learning to track and rope a mechanical steer begins exactly the same as learning with a dummy. Here, Zeb Allen practices riding to the proper position and throwing his rope. This allows him to learn the angle that his throw needs to be and how it feels to rope off a horse.*

7.4 *Heelers have two positions to learn: hazing and catching. Hazing, or keeping the steer running in a straight path down the arena, gives the header a clean shot at catching. The hazing position is 10 feet to the right of the steer, with the horse's nose about even with the steer's tail, as Joshua Hawkins demonstrates here with a live steer during a practice. Later, he will change positions and put his horse's nose even with the steer's left hip, about 6 inches away, in preparation for his catch.*

Both Rickey Green and Speed Williams teach their students to track a steer on horseback at a trot. This is because the trot is a rougher gait to ride and encourages an independent seat. Ropers then find tracking easier to duplicate at the faster lope, which is smoother.

However, the process of learning to track a steer actually begins on the ground, when you are roping the dummy and learning to position for the throw by walking to your target (see chapter 5, p. 89). On the horse, the procedure is much the same. You ride to the correct position in relation to the steer before attempting to throw.

The proper position for the *header* is about 3 or 4 feet to the left of a steer, with your horse's nose even with the steer's right hip bone (fig. 7.3). The *heeler* has two positions to learn when tracking: The first job in any run is to *haze,* or keep the steer running in a straight path down the arena, so the header can get a clean shot. During that time, the heeler needs to be about 10 feet—or a horse-length-and-a-half—to the right of the steer with the horse's nose no further forward than the steer's tail (fig. 7.4). After the header catches and turns the steer left into what is called the *corner,* the heeler should put his horse's

nose even with the steer's left hip, about 6 inches away. This position sets the heeler up in an ideal location to make his catch.

7.5 *Once you can ride, rope a dummy, and track a mechanical or live steer properly through every stage of the run, it is time to bring it all together.*

## READY TO ROPE: BRINGING IT ALL TOGETHER

Once you can ride, rope a dummy, and track a mechanical or live steer properly through every stage of the run, it is time bring it all together, and combine the three actions (fig. 7.5).

### Catching a Mechanical Steer

It is up to you to use your previous lessons when learning how to catch a steer in motion. However, Rickey Green and Speed Williams have some tips for getting the most from a mechanical steer at this stage.

Williams' first consideration is safety. If you have one of the types of machines that are towed, be aware of what is used to pull it. A light all-terrain vehicle (ATV), like a four-wheeler, is best, rather than some of the heavier ATVs that are popular today. In many cases, a heel horse can stop a light ATV; however, a larger vehicle, when the driver is holding the gas pedal down, can't be stopped with a rope and this can cause problems.

Someone experienced should be at the controls of the mechanical steer. He needs to pay attention and be aware of when to slow or stop to avoid trouble, especially after you catch. This person can also play a big role in your training: He can increase the challenge by changing variables like speed and the angle of the turn in a run. Or, he can set up situations that might come up with a live steer, such as veering off pattern to the right.

*Roping from Horseback*

*7.6 Once you can catch, you then must then learn to dally. Here, Rickey Green demonstrates proper technique, with his thumb rolled out of sight, down alongside the rest of his fingers. He says that many ropers learn to dally with their thumb in the air, which can be dangerous.*

Once you can catch, you must then learn to *dally* (fig. 7.6). Green says that many ropers are misinformed about the proper technique—they learn to dally with their thumb in the air, which is the perfect position to get that thumb caught in the coil. The thumb side of the dallying hand should be facing the sky, but the thumb itself should be rolled down and hidden alongside the nails of the rest of the fingers.

To help inexperienced ropers learn this, Williams instructs his students to only carry a single coil when they first start catching and dallying. Later, when all the maneuvers are automatic and you are more confident in your ability to perform every one of them consistently, you can progress to using a full-length rope.

Although taking a knife to a new rope might seem counterproductive, a single coil teaches beginning ropers how to catch efficiently because they don't have the luxury of dropping coils for added length. This is also a preventive safety measure, because with a longer rope there is increased risk of tangling your hand when dallying. A shorter rope simply eases your responsibility by giving you less to hold onto until you are ready for it.

## Roping Live Cattle

Once you can catch your mechanical dummy consistently 10 to 15 times in a row, you are ready to take on a live steer. Believe it or not, every technique is exactly the same on a live steer as it is on the mechanical kind. It is a good idea to start out with slower, more seasoned cattle rather than fresh, young steers (fig. 7.7). Cattle that are too frisky can be too much of a challenge for a beginner.

By the time you graduate to live cattle, the actions required to catch as a header or heeler should be automatic. If this is the case, then the transition should be fairly easy, with the learning curve being related to learning to gauge how an unpredictable animal will react in each situation.

# THE IDEAL RUN

The basic mechanics of a correct team roping run are covered in chapter 1 (p. 14). Here we'll review the phases of the run, and I'll share some tips for headers and heelers to create the best run possible. Each stage is important and must go well for the following sequence to happen.

## Breaking from the Box

First, both riders must leave the box to begin a run. This is the most dangerous location inside an arena and many things can go wrong here. Novices should not attempt learning to break from the box alone.

Factors like feel, balance, and the temperament of the horse come into play in a roping box. It can be compared to the starting gate of a racetrack. This is where a professional instructor can help. Green says that some of the most intricate work at his roping schools is done in the box, teaching people how to get out of the box safely. Also, a well-trained horse can help you stay safe as you learn this leg of the event. A seasoned competitor knows how to break correctly and softly from the box, and only then build speed toward the steer.

Entering the run, the header and heeler chase the steer from its left and right sides, respectively. (Review the exact positioning for each rider through the run beginning on p. 16.) According to the *USTRC Rulebook*, the team is only allowed two loops—two chances—to catch a steer, so accuracy is very important.

## Catching

The header is the first one to attempt to catch; however, the heeler is a big part of a header's success. The heeler's job doesn't begin when the header turns the steer. In fact, the heeler is immediately called to action, hazing the steer. His job is to keep the steer running in a predictable, straight line so the header has the best shot possible.

As mentioned earlier in the book, and according to the official *USTRC Rulebook*, for a header there are three legal catches: (1) around both horns, (2) around the neck, and (3) around half a head, which is similar to a neck catch, except one horn is within the loop and the other outside of it.

As soon as the header catches, he dallies and turns the steer left. This part of the run is called the *corner*. A smooth action on the part of the header sets the steer up for the heeler to make his shot. Ideally, the steer's hind legs continue with forward motion in a gentle curve that swings them out to the right.

In modern roping, the header wants to slow a steer down gradually and guide it left, keeping him hopping in a smooth semicircle that gives the heeler a quicker, better shot (fig. 7.8). When the header leads a steer, he should be watching the steer but also be aware of the heeler's loop.

7.8 *Ideally, the header guides the steer in a smooth semicircle, rather than a sudden jerk left. Doing so gives the heeler the best chance to catch because the steer moves with rhythm.*

At the same time, the heeler should look inside at the steer's left hind leg as he prepares to throw. The heeler should also be positioned as mentioned earlier in this chapter (p. 110), with his horse's nose about 6 inches away from the steer's left hip.

After catching, the heeler dallies best when he turns his coils sideways, with his knuckles forward. Both of his elbows should rise when he wraps his rope. This coordinated set of motions should look something like a driver turning the steering wheel of his vehicle.

While the heeler is dallying, the header should be watching him, timing when to *face*. After the two riders face each other and the steer is caught between two taut ropes, the run is finished, and in competition, the flagger drops his flag.

*Roping from Horseback*

*7.9 Good manners begin
in the box, according to
Clinton Anderson. Horses
should remain alert but
calm, like these two, and
wait for their rider's signal
before breaking out.*

Penalties can add to the team's time (as covered in chapter 1, p. 18), such as either roper leaving the box before the steer has traveled the distance of its allotted headstart. A 5-second penalty is added to the team's total time for this infraction. Also, if a heeler only catches a single hind foot, the penalty is 5 extra seconds. If either roper misses completely, it is grounds for disqualification and the team receives "no time."

## THINK OUTSIDE THE BOX

What if your horse is the team member preventing you from having a picture-perfect run? Sometimes, horse experience can work against you, as seasoned athletes may know their job too well and anticipate. Or, they just get excited and stop listening.

Good manners begin in the box, according to Clinton Anderson (fig. 7.9). Incidentally, this is where many runs fall apart before they begin. A good start is the first step toward a successful finish. That sounds obvious, but more than likely, by this point you've seen ropers at every level of the sport get a poor start by struggling with a horse that's antsy, tossing his head, rearing, and being disrespectful in other ways toward the rider, instead of focusing on the run ahead.

When the steer is released, you've got precious little time to get your horse focused on his job so that you can do yours. In a sport where split-second decisions make or break a run, you don't have long to worry about getting the horse to direct his attention to you and listen to your cues.

According to Anderson, the primary cause of bad behavior in the box is the horse associating it with blowing out of it at a full gallop. Soon, the horse learns his job and stops listening to the rider for the cue. In response, most riders tend to pull on the reins and try to hold the horse still, which usually only results in a more explosive reaction from the horse.

To fix a box-sour problem, Anderson advises you go back to the lessons for softening the five body parts (beginning on p. 100), and practice them in the box. The familiar exercises should snap your horse's attention back to you and redirect his excited energy. In particular, he suggests that you work on bending through the rib cage, where the horse travels a small circle with his entire body curved. This not only gives the horse's feet somewhere to go, it also softens and lowers his head, which is most likely high when the horse is fidgety in the box.

Another method Anderson uses for developing a calm roping horse is to make the box the only place in the arena that the horse can relax. Soon, the horse can't wait to stand quietly. In other words, make the wrong thing hard, and the right thing easy! He suggests working the horse hard outside the box until he's sweaty and huffing and puffing a bit, then take him inside the box to let him catch his breath (fig. 7.10). His theory is that horses are basically lazy creatures, and it won't take long for one to decide that the box isn't such a bad place after all. Then, the horse begins to associate the box with rest and the arena with hard work.

*7.10  If your horse is fidgety in the box, Anderson suggests making it the only place he can relax and cool off from a hard workout. This sweaty horse enters the box calmly after steady exercise worked out any extra excitement.*

## RATING YOUR RUN

Another performance issue Anderson sees many seasoned roping horses develop is a bad "cruise control." He says that trying to control a horse while roping is hard enough, without having to deal with one that tends to fight. So, he offers a couple of drills to reinforce to your horse that he needs to listen to your instructions during the run.

7.11 *Practice makes perfect when sharpening your horse's rate, especially if he has bad "cruise control." The first step is to track loose steers around the arena, which is not a bad idea as a refresher course for any horse.*

First, refresh *rate*—or speed control—by simply tracking a loose steer around the arena (fig. 7.11). This exercise is identical to the final exam used earlier in this chapter when evaluating students' readiness to rope from horseback (p. 110). Like the earlier drill, it is also best when initially performed at the trot. Anything faster could excite your horse too much.

More than likely, when you first start this exercise, Anderson says that your horse will break into a canter and charge the steer because he is in the habit of ignoring you and setting his own agenda. When he does go faster than you want, he advises to let the horse commit to the mistake for a stride or two. Then, sit down and pull your horse off the steer by drawing him to a stop and backing him up.

Each time you begin to track the steer, be sure to give your horse plenty of rein and a chance to commit to the mistake, rather than anticipating and trying to prevent a slip-up. Also, don't let the horse get away with misbehaving too long before correcting him.

7.12 *Anderson says that in moderation, drills help focus a horse, like the two shown here, but don't dampen his drive to work.*

Although at first it sounds counterproductive, try practicing this drill with your horse until you almost have to push him to follow the steer. Ropers don't need to worry about ruining their horses, says Anderson, because as soon as that horse is in the box, he will perk up and get excited again. Hopefully, it will be with a bit more rate.

After the horse can rate with a loose steer, return the horse to the box. There, release steers without chasing them, or *score*. Even though the horse may have started to understand the concept of not charging after the cow, when he gets in the box and sees the steer go, he'll usually revert to ignoring you. That's perfectly normal—you just have to help him work through it.

To get the most out of this portion of the lesson, Anderson says to carry a rope in your hand to make the scenario realistic for your horse. Remember, you're not keeping the horse from making a mistake. You're just setting up the situation and letting him commit to the mistake. This is where the drills to calm

*Roping from Horseback*

a horse in the box can come in handy yet again to refocus the horse's attention on you, instead of fixating on the breaking steer.

However, you have to find a balance so that you have a horse that listens to you, but still loves his job and is good at it (fig. 7.12). Anderson says that most roping horses have so much natural steer instinct that it would be relatively hard to train them to the extent that they don't have the desire to chase one.

## READY FOR THE ROAD

Once you have the basic procedure of roping under your belt, catching live cattle has become familiar, and your horse is listening well through every stage of the run, you may be curious to see how your skills stack up against other ropers of your level. There's only one way to find out. Check out Part Three to learn how to "get in the game."

# Competition

# GETTING IN THE GAME

YOU FINALLY ARE READY to "take your new skills to town," and see how you stack up against other team ropers in competition (fig. 8.1). This chapter helps you navigate the necessary paperwork, find a suitable debut roping event, and gives you some additional tips for success before you hit the road.

The first two items on your to-do list are joining the USTRC and getting classified (ability ranking). You can take care of both well before the competition you plan on participating in—or even on the day that you rope (fig. 8.2). The USTRC membership forms are available in every issue of the *SuperLooper Magazine* as well as onsite at the roping office of every sanctioned and affiliate event. Any producer—or event coordinator—who is following the USTRC's guidelines is able and encouraged to sell memberships at his or her competitions.

8.1 *Once you are confident in the saddle and in your roping skills, giving competition a shot is a great way to track your progress.*

8.2 *The first two items on your to-do list when you are ready to compete are joining the USTRC and getting classified (your numerical ability ranking). You can take care of both before the competition or on the day that you rope, like this roper is doing here. Note that at most events you must locate the show secretary's table, as she won't come find you!*

## USTRC MEMBERSHIP

While you are training in preparation for eventual competition, membership in the USTRC is a good idea. When you are ready for the spotlight, it becomes essential (fig. 8.3).

Membership comes with a rich set of benefits. Most importantly, it allows you to join the larger team roping community. Every new (and renewing) member receives a welcome packet after their purchase, which includes a listing of USTRC benefits for their membership option, a membership card, and an official window decal. In addition, you can also expect to find promotional items from sponsors, which may include discounts for their products and services.

8.3 *While you are training, membership in the USTRC is a good idea. When you are ready for the spotlight, it becomes essential. Membership comes with a rich set of benefits. Most importantly, it allows you to join the larger team roping community.*

The USTRC offers a few different membership options, based on your needs, age, and geographic location. Pricing options range from free youth membership, which is for those who are 12 and under, to $300 annually for the premium membership package. Additional family memberships can be purchased at a discounted price. Details for each type of membership can be found at www.ustrc.com.

## CLASSIFICATIONS

Once you have chosen and applied for membership, you will be given a temporary numerical classification by the USTRC. There are a few first-time member questions that USTRC Classification personnel or event producers will ask to help gauge an applicant's ability (fig. 8.4). They cover topics such as how long an applicant has been roping; how long competing; how consistent at catching steers in succession; and the applicant's history competing with non-USTRC team roping organizations. Several independent associations exist, mostly on the local and regional level.

As explained in chapter 1 (p. 22) the USTRC ranks *headers* on a nine-point numeric scale, and *heelers* on a 10-point scale. Lower-numbered ropers are the least experienced and the highest ones are at a professional level. Numbers 1 through 6 are rated the same for both headers and heelers. Once you reach upper amateur and professional levels, the meaning of each rating differs slightly for the two positions.

The *USTRC Rulebook* states that all initial classifications are temporary until randomly selected ropers vote on your ranking via ballots or you have accumulated solid performance data, whichever comes first. From there, your number is raised, lowered, or left the same based on what you do in competition.

### Fine-Tuning Classifications

The USTRC's Team Roping Information and Data (TRIAD) classification system was refined in 2010 to further level your playing field (see more about TRIAD on p. 22). According to the *Rulebook,* a classification system is used to limit the margin of error when setting roping divisions. Within some of these levels, higher-end amateur and professional ropers may also be assigned the designation of "Elite." An example given in the *USTRC Rulebook* is a #5 header who has proven to have a competitive advantage amongst other #5 headers, but is not ready for a full number increase to a 6. That person would be reclassified up to an Elite #5. Also, a #5 header who has proven to struggle at that level, but would be too dominant as a #4, would be reclassified down to an Elite #4.

The classification system affords ropers of every skill level the opportunity to be competitive by accurately grouping them with other ropers of like skill.

8.4  *Speed Williams strongly suggests that you practice dealing with mental pressure at home before the big day. He explains that doing so minimizes your stress and jitters during the main event.*

## FINDING A COMPETITION

Once you are a card-carrying, classified USTRC member, you are ready to enter a roping. If you haven't already, now is the time to find a place to compete. Team ropings are all the same, right? Unfortunately, this is not the case. Some are definitely better than others. But, don't worry. If you follow the advice outlined below, you are sure to locate a great one that fits you.

To find an event in your area, a great starting point is to visit USTRC's calendar of events on its website (www.ustrc.com). There, you will find a schedule of *sanctioned*, *affiliate* and *non-sanctioned* (not recognized by USTRC) events, which is constantly updated. Another good reading reference is *SuperLooper Magazine.* Every USTRC-sanctioned or affiliate event advertisement has a specific logo at the top that clearly designates what type of competition it is promoting. In addition to event advertisements, a calendar of events can be found in each issue (fig. 8.5).

Team roping events are held all over the United States, even in far-flung locations. From Maui to New York, the USTRC hosts events in every region. There is sure to be a sanctioned or affiliate event near you.

Another resource for finding a local event is to ask around, according to Rickey Green. Ask fellow ropers from your hometown where they go to compete. Or, if you have been attending a public practice or taking lessons, you will often hear about upcoming events in the course of everyday conversation. Look for printed announcements posted at your local arenas.

A big part of your decision if a roping is worth your time and money is to find a producer who has a great reputation. Again, word-of-mouth comes into play. Talk to other team ropers. They are sure to have certain ropings that they will not miss. Others, they make a point to steer clear of if possible.

Or, if you know of an upcoming roping, just visit the event. This is especially easy if it is a weekly or monthly occurrence. When you arrive, there are several things to look for during your visit that will help you decide whether to compete there in the future:

- Observe the roping from the stands. Does it appear to be fairly run? Or, do you notice bias in the system? Some producers don't respect or use the number system, and entrants are placed into an unlevel playing field.

- Listen to the competitors' reactions to the day's events. They will often provide the most immediate feedback about the way the competition is being managed. Of course, keep in mind these are individual opinions. What you need to pay attention to are reoccurring sentiments, rather than a single statement. If you hear a universal feeling amongst the competition crowd, that should be noted.

8.5 *To find a team roping in your area, a good starting place is SuperLooper Magazine, USTRC's official publication, which comes free with your membership. Inside, events are advertised and a calendar is included in each issue. Or, visit USTRC's calendar of events page on its website—www.ustrc.com.*

Leave your seat to check out the facilities. Restrooms should be clean, parking should be plentiful, and food and beverage concessions available. Most importantly, the ground inside the arena should be in adequate condition and, above all, safe. For example, it should be free of rocks and trash.

Do remember not to grade too harshly when visiting your local roping. Like many activities in the horse and other hobby industries, producers don't usually get rich by hosting team ropings. Most of the time, their motivation is the opportunity to make a positive impact on the area's roping community and to build new friendships with other enthusiasts. If the day's spectators and competitors seem happy overall with the event, although it may have a few minor infractions, trust their opinions. Join in next time, and have some fun with them (fig. 8.6).

## USTRC Competition

In addition to your local team roping jackpots, you should also definitely consider dipping your toe in the waters of a competition produced by the United States Team Roping Championships, regardless of your level of skill. These *sanctioned events* are an experience that is a step above the typical gathering. However, don't let the top-of-the-line accommodations intimidate you. Each one features multiple divisions that welcome everyone from the most novice roper to the elite seasoned competitor and, as mentioned before, allows for a level

8.6 *When visiting a team roping to see if it is right for you, notice how the other team ropers and spectators feel about the event. If they are enjoying themselves and are happy with the competition, maybe you should consider joining them the next time.*

Team Roping 101

playing field for all. The USTRC strives to create a place for everyone to test their abilities against those of similarly talented peers.

When you arrive at a USTRC roping, you will find that it features deep competitor benefits and top-notch customer service for its entrants. These are the two major qualities that set sanctioned ropings apart from other events. Whether you enter in Washington State or Washington D.C., you should find the same air of professionalism, and elite awards, cattle, and staff.

The USTRC doesn't provide this elevated experience by happenstance. First, their producers lay the groundwork with extensive preparation. They hire professional staff, like announcers and flaggers, and judges. They also work to secure superior cattle, which provide the proper challenge for each division. When selecting facilities, they search out those indoors, with ample stalling. Covered arenas provide more consistent opportunities for each team, as weather is not a factor.

Once staff and facilities are in place, the producers take time to consider other touches—like ensuring that the ground will be consistently maintained from run to run and how the sponsors' banners are placed along the arena walls. The banners dress up the arena fences and, at the same time, give recognition to the corporate partners who support team roping.

Spectators and exhibitors will notice other small luxuries that separate USTRC team ropings apart from others. Well-trained secretaries and other administrative staff, who can capably provide topnotch customer service at every step to guide you from entering to collecting awards, will be among the first to greet you. The schedule is punctual and precise, so entrants know exactly what time the roping will kick off and the order of events. The schedule is formatted for the comfort of participants. For example, it is tailored to limit late-night hours. If possible, this is accomplished by using multiple arenas to speed along each division timeframe.

Another reason to attend USTRC-sanctioned team ropings is the superb quality of the awards they give to winning entrants in each division. Not only can top competitors walk away with big cash in their pockets, many also leave with prizes like Martin Saddlery trophy saddles (www.martinsaddlery. com) and Gist Silversmiths championship belt buckles (www.gistsilversmiths. com). Both manufacturers are known industry-wide for the excellence in craftsmanship that their talented artists provide.

These are just a few examples of the consistent, quality experience that team ropers can expect to find at USTRC-produced events.


## PREPPING FOR SUCCESS

Once you have located some events to attend and have your paperwork in order, it's time to hit the road. Before you leave, here are some tips from Speed Williams that could make the journey less stressful:

*Pack early* and prepare for *anything* (fig. 8.7). Store your gear at all times in your trailer, so it is ready to go when you are, or if this isn't an option for you, try to load as much as possible the night before you leave.

Although you may never need it, remember to *bring extras of important equipment*—especially ropes. Even if you are a careful planner, it is not a matter of if, but when, you will forget an item. According to Williams, this isn't just a worry for novices. Forgetfulness is just as likely to strike professionals who travel frequently. Extra gear can also be a lifesaver if something breaks or wears out while you are on the road. It eliminates the stress of finding a way to quickly replace the defective item.

Be ready to ride an hour before the roping is scheduled to start. That way, if the roping is ahead of schedule you'll be "on," and if you happened to forget something, you have a chance to figure out a solution (fig. 8.8).

Like your horse, you are an athlete and should fuel your body with the energy it needs to compete. So, be sure to bring healthy snacks that sustain you throughout the day.

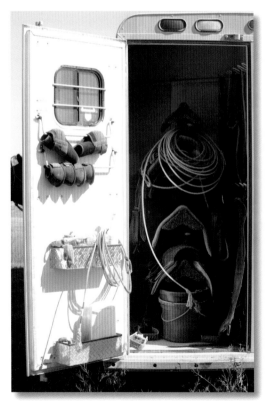

8.7 *Pack early and pack extra before hitting the road, according to Speed Williams. Doing so reduces stress on your big day. He adds that forgetfulness doesn't only strike novices, and that extra gear can be a lifesaver when something wears out or breaks on the road.*

## COST-CUTTING TIPS

While any sport involves certain expenses, there are always ways to make enjoying it a bit more economical. "Trailer-pooling" is a great cost-cutting option for many team ropers who can arrange to travel together. That, along with bringing your own drinks, snacks, and meals can significantly cut down on your total expenses.

Ropers, particularly those new to the sport, can prioritize the fun of the sport over winning big by choosing to patronize events that offer minimal entry fees or other low-cost options to make competing more economical. However you trim your budget, be sure to see what deals individual producers offer in your area. In addition to these general ideas, many local producers may also offer you some extra perks—just for being new.

8.8 *Be ready to ride an hour before the roping is scheduled to start. This accommodates any fluctuations in the schedule and allows you to troubleshoot problems—such as forgotten or broken equipment—before you're under the wire.*

# YOUR FIRST COMPETITION

YOU'VE MADE IT. All your hard work has built up to this, your first competition (fig. 9.1). You have spent enough time studying the sport, strengthening your riding skills, and practicing your rope-handling so that you feel comfortable with the "Big Day."

You should have all your paperwork in order (see p. 123). According to the *USTRC Rulebook*, participation in an approved event without a valid membership card or application results in disqualification of you and your partner, even if the partner has an up-to-date card. Disqualified ropers forfeit entry money, prizes, and payout earnings. So, it's important—do not forget it!

Other documents to remember are your horse's required travel, health, and registration paperwork. Be sure to research your municipal, county/parish, or state requirements before heading out. For example, in many states, a negative Coggins certificate from a licensed veterinarian must accompany a trailered horse. This test checks for the highly transmittable and deadly Equine Infectious Anemia (EIA) antibodies (fig. 9.2).

9.1 *Welcome to your first team roping! Competition is a great way to compare your abilities with those of other team ropers—and to have some fun.*

9.2 *Be sure to research your municipal, county/parish, or state requirements before heading out. For example, in many states, a negative Coggins certificate from a licensed veterinarian must accompany a trailered horse. This test checks for the highly transmittable and deadly Equine Infectious Anemia (EIA) antibodies.*

# DRESS CODE

For USTRC competition, keep in mind that a dress code does apply when competing, and that disqualification is possible for failure to comply (fig. 9.3). Ropers must wear a cowboy hat or no hat at all. Caps are not allowed inside the arena, nor are they permitted to be tied on, or attached in any way to you or your equipment during the course of a run. Cowboy Western attire is required, which includes shirts with a sewn-on collar and a full-buttoned front styling, with short or long sleeves. Sleeveless shirts are not legal. As far as footwear, Western boots, or approved laced cowboy shoes with a heel are required. Unless a medical exemption is made, no other heeled footwear or type of tennis shoe is permitted.

*9.3 While this heeler's attire is perfectly acceptable for the practice he is at, when it comes time for competition, he will need a long-sleeved shirt with a collar and a Western hat instead of his ball cap.*

## SIGNING UP

Your first task upon arrival at an event is to locate the event secretary's desk. The same person who helps you purchase a membership, if needed, can also take care of your entry and any questions. There will always be two or more event secretaries who process entries. At least one of them will deal with the public, while one or more are behind the scenes, entering the information into a computer and filing forms or payments. At the conclusion of each division's competition, this same staff also calculates payouts and prizes. If you do well, this is where you come to be awarded your winnings.

An early arrival allows plenty of time for you to show required documents, enter, mentally prepare, and warm up your horse. Entry deadlines for each division can vary, but plan on having your entries complete at least an hour before your division, or roping level, is scheduled to start.

The only exception to this rule for entry deadlines applies to USTRC Gold Plus members. These ropers can pre-enter any USTRC-sanctioned event beforehand by calling th Gold Plus representative. All other membership levels must enter onsite the day of the roping, with the exception of Regional and National Finals, which require pre-entry.

Affiliate event timeframes are at the discretion of the individual producers, so be sure to read the event advertisements closely beforehand and listen to the loudspeaker announcements at the event to learn about entry cutoff times.

When you pay for your entries, you must have cash. Checks are only accepted from Gold Plus members at USTRC events. Many producers of all types of team ropings do not handle credit or debit cards at their events. Therefore, ropers should be sure to bring along enough cash to cover their transactions for that day, just in case. The one exception is when you make a separate membership purchase. For those, checks are always accepted. Most producers will include payment information in their advertising. The ad will state whether or not the event is cash only and if it will accept checks from only Gold Plus members.

Budget accordingly. Be optimistic, but realistic about your abilities and spend only the amount of money you are prepared to leave there. While the payback is often generous, it is not guaranteed.

## GETTING YOUR DRAW

Once you have entered and the books have closed, it is time to learn when you will be roping. That is determined by a computer "draw," which randomly assigns you a team number for each of your entries. It is a good idea to write your team number or numbers down. That way, you know when you are up. And, announcers can use either your name or team number to call you to the box.

Your draw lists the order in which you will rope, and, if there are *rotations* in your division, which rotation you are in. Rotations are used at many events, especially larger ones with hundreds or thousands of teams, to streamline the action. This USTRC innovation has substantially reduced the amount of time it takes a team to complete its roping runs.

Here's how it works: Each rotation in a division is usually made up of either 50 or 75 teams. Every team in a rotation will complete all of its runs, except the *short go round*—the final round that determines the winners—before the next rotation, or group of ropers, begins. This allows all the teams that did not catch on one of their runs, and were thus eliminated from competition, to go on about their business.

Only those teams that caught all their steers will remain to see if their cumulative time will be fast enough to beat the "cutoff time" and qualify them for the short go round. Usually, only the top 20 to 30 teams from the previous rounds make the short go round. The cutoff time is cumulative and is determined by the slowest team that is eligible to compete in the short go round. So, the current cutoff time could drop progressively lower, as teams in later rotations beat that time, bumping that slowest team out of the competition.

The rotation concept has saved countless hours of ropers endlessly waiting for their time to rope. Previously, if you were team number 1 with 250 teams to go, for example, you would rope your first steer and wait for every one of the other teams to take its run before you would rope your second steer. Then, you would wait once more each time you were successful in catching your steer while all the other returning teams that caught their first steer roped their second round.

With rotations, you know fairly quickly whether you are one of the few that might qualify for the short go round, or one of the teams that can either go home or find something else to do while waiting for the next division you have entered to begin.

In regards to the draw, it is important to realize that you don't need to know any other competitors to enter a team roping as a novice. The USTRC entry software, which is used at many events, is very sophisticated, and can choose all your partners for you. This can be a great way to meet other ropers.

Later, when you get to know more team ropers, you have the option of choosing one or more of your teammates. Keep in mind that, according to the *USTRC Rulebook*, no two ropers may compete twice together in any single division at an event. This includes switching ends as header and heeler.

When entries are complete, the event secretary will print out an alphabet-ized roster, which is posted in a designated area. You can walk up and easily find out who your partners are and your team numbers. Then, you just need to be ready to compete when your name or number is called.

## MENTAL PREPARATION

Being mentally prepared to compete takes practice at home. But practicing at home can be vastly different from competing for the first time in an unfamiliar arena and being watched by hundreds of people.

Speed Williams advises that you do what you can to mimic competition conditions in the practice pen by inviting others to rope with you, visiting other roper's practice pens, and entering small local events, all of which are less stressful than the "real deal."

Even when simply practicing or roping with friends for fun, he says that you should try to bring a level of adrenalin to every run, motivating yourself to focus and make each run a success. Accomplish this by incorporating a high-stakes practice into your schedule. The setup can be a simple bet between teammates, where the loser has to unsaddle and groom the winner's horse at the end of practice. Practicing like this will stimulate the nerves in the practice pen and make it easier for you to deal with the pressure of competition. Simply put, the more pressure you can handle at home, the less it will bother you when it counts.

Although you may have practiced every conceivable scenario at home, your first competition is bound to bring on a few jitters. The unknown is scary to everyone, but if you're prepared, you have to trust that your knowledge and training will carry you through (fig. 9.4).

## PHYSICAL PREPARATION

While mental preparation is key to having success, so too is physical preparation for both you and your horse, according to Williams. The process of warming up your horse before you rope will usually get you ready at the same time.

Like people, every horse is different. Williams' rule is that his horse is both mentally and physically set to compete when the horse breaks a sweat. It's important that every rider knows the limitations of his horse and warms him up appropriately. An overly tired horse won't have the energy to perform later and a horse not warmed up enough won't do well either. Understanding how to prepare your individual horse for competition will only come from spending time with him at home in the practice arena.

Keep in mind that your horse has a left and right side and both sides need to be trained (fig. 9.5). At almost any team roping, you can observe ropers loping their horses to the left and rarely will you see a horse being worked to the right. According to Williams, many ropers incorrectly believe that the run is based on left turns and the horse needs to run the pattern on the left lead. So, many ropers don't see the benefit of developing the right half of the horse.

9.4 *Practice every conceivable scenario at home, says Speed Williams, so when you are faced with the same challenges during competition—like this steer that drags his hind feet— you will have the experience to know how to deal with them.*

*9.5 At many team ropings, riders only warm their horses up with left-hand circles; however, Speed Williams says it is important to also ride right circles, like this rider, to balance the development and readiness of muscles on both sides of your horse's body, in case little-used muscles are suddenly called on, such as when a steer darts off to the right.*

Balancing the training to both the left and right side will help the horse's muscles strengthen uniformly. And, your horse will develop the ability to remain supple and light on the bit. By this point, your horse should be well in control, and warming up all the muscles allows him to respond in any situation. For example, should the steer dart right in the run, your horse will be able to switch to the right lead to chase after it.

9.6 *Remember, your first event is primarily about learning and having fun. Don't put too much pressure on yourself or your horse until you "learn the ropes" of competition.*

## COMPETING

When your number or name is called, that's it. Hopefully, you have practiced sufficiently at home, prepared enough during your warm-up, and are lucky enough to have drawn good partners and easy steers.

Good luck, and have fun! Remember, your goal the first day isn't to place first (fig. 9.6). Your objective is to simply show up and test your skills. Anything extra is icing on the cake!

*Your First Competition*

# 10

# LESSON LEARNED

WHETHER YOU GO HOME with a paycheck or not, you can now call yourself a competitive team roper (fig. 10.1). That is no small thing. Although your primary goal should have been to learn the process of entering and competing in a team roping event, how did your study-time and training prepare you when compared to those of other ropers at your level?

You should now know your strong points and a few things you can work on in practice. Maybe you or your horse needs additional athletic conditioning to gain a bit more of an edge. Maybe you just need more time to become proficient at the skills you already know. Or, maybe the day went by in such a frenzied blur that you don't know how you ended up placing the way you did.

That is why Speed Williams says that for your first competition, and indeed, every competition, you should have someone in the stands recording your run on a video camera or cell phone. Don't just listen to what others say about your runs. Watch the video and see if you agree with what others are telling you. Many times, they will have noticed things you didn't. It may have looked different from their angle of sight, or because they were not directly and emotionally involved with the run.

Regardless of how you placed, I hope you have enjoyed the journey from the bleachers to the box enough to keep on going (fig. 10.2). You know the basic mechanics of what it takes to be a team roper, now you just need to practice them.

10.1 *Hopefully, you enjoyed yourself enough at your first event to enter another. Congratulations! Give yourself and your horse a well-deserved rest and pat on the back.*

10.2 *Now that you are a team roper, you are part of the generations of cowboys and cowgirls who have practiced the art since the earliest ranching days, when they set out to gather cattle from the range. Hopefully you enjoyed your journey from the bleachers to the box enough to keep on going.*

# About the Contributors

For in-depth knowledge about team roping, contact a professional instructor, such as Rickey Green or Speed Williams, who were kind enough to lend their expertise for this book. Both of them, and many other team roping professionals, have excellent websites, videos and other resource material to educate beginner-to-advanced enthusiasts. Many also tour the country to reach ropers across the nation.

Learn about RICKEY GREEN and the educational opportunities he offers at www.powerteamroping.com. There, members can watch a new video each month and participate in a blog where they can interact with Green and have individual questions answered. A list of upcoming schools and details about scheduling lessons are also provided.

Details about SPEED WILLIAMS can be found at www.speedroping.com. Visitors have a wide selection of subscriber-based and free videos to choose from that offers deep coverage of many team roping topics. You can also find information about Williams' upcoming schools and other educational opportunities on the site.

For more on the horsemanship skills that can prepare you and your horse for the sport of team roping, visit CLINTON ANDERSON'S website at www.downunderhorsemanship.com. Anderson is a well-known clinician and horse trainer, and co-author of several books, including *Clinton Anderson's Downunder Horsemanship: Establishing Respect and Control for English and Western Riders* and *Clinton Anderson's Lessons Well Learned: Why My Method Works for Any Horse.*

For more information about USTRC and team roping, the main office, headquartered in Stephenville, Texas, may be contacted with your general questions and comments:

Phone: 254.968.0002
E-mail: ustrc@ustrc.com
Website: www.ustrc.com

- The Roping Entry Department handles inquiries and services about pre-entry event status and changes to existing entries: central-entry@ustrc.com.

- If you are a new member and need to be classified or a renewing member with a question regarding your handicap number status, double numbers, membership card replacement, or delivery status and other general classification questions, contact the Classifications Department: classifications@ustrc.com.

- If you are a Gold Plus member, contact your representative for assistance about membership status, family member changes, stall reservations, and general questions: goldplus@ustrc.com.

# Bibliography

Anderson, Clinton. Personal interview. 25 Aug 2010

AQHA. *2010 AQHA Rule Book*. Web. 10 June 2010.

Baldwin, Peter. Personal interview. 26 July 2010.

Beeman, Marvin DVM. *Conformation: The Relationship of Form to Function*. No date given, circa 1996. Reprint from the *Quarter Horse Journal*.

Bray, Craig. Personal interview. 28 June 2010.

Bray, Ken. Personal interview. 26 June 2010.

Bray, Kirk. Personal interview. 26 June 2010.

Clements, Ben. Personal interview. 3 August 2010.

Conklin, Brit, DVM. Personal interview. 25 February 2010.

Dawes, Judy. Personal interview. 15 May 2010.

Dorris, Dustin, DVM. Personal interview. 25 April 2010.

ESPN. http://sports.espn.go.com/rodeo/news/story?id=4736394. Web. Dec 12, 2009.

Findlay, John. Personal interview. 15 May 2010.

Green, Rickey. Personal interview. 20 June 2010.

Lane, Kim. Personal interview. 22 July 2010.

Lucero, Ferron. Personal interview. 15 May 2010.

NRCHA. Press release. 25 February 2008.

Osburn, Kathie. Personal interview. 24 June 2010.

Peterson, Tracey. Personal interview. 26 June 2010.

Poythress, Gary. Personal interview. 15 May 2010.

Price, Stephen D. *The American Quarter Horse.* Lyons Press.

USTRC. *2010 USTRC Rulebook*. www.ustrc.com. Web. 10 June 2010.

Williams, Speed. Personal interview. 20 June 2010.

# Index

Gray horses, health considerations, 78
Green, Rickey, 43, *43*, 93
Grip, on rope, 83–84, *85*
Ground handling skills, 98–99, *98–99*
Ground money, 7
Groundwork, for ropers. *See* Roper
  groundwork
Gullet, of saddle, 51, *51*

Halters, 99–100, 101
Hand and finger position, 84, *85*, 87, 112
Handicap system. *See* Classification ratings
Hazing, 7, 110, 114
Head and headset. *See also* Tie-downs
  conformation and, 77–78
  softness drills for, 102, *103*
Head catches, 7, 114
Head-ducking, 7
Header barriers, 4
Headers
  about, 7, 16
  classification ratings, 22–23
  legal catches, 114
  position in saddle, *49*
  practice dummies for, 89–90
  rope selection, 35, 39
  throwing angle, 87
  tracking position, 88, 110, *110*
Heading horses, 7, 59, *59*, 73, 76
Headstalls, 7, 60
Heats, 8, 138–139
Heel catches, 8
Heelers
  about, 8, 16
  classification ratings, 22–23
  penalties, 18
  position in saddle, *49*
  practice dummies for, 89–90
  rope selection, 35–37, *36*, 39
  throwing angle, 87
  tracking position, 88, 110, *110*
Heeling horses, 8, *60*, 73, 76
Hereditary Equine Regional Dermal
  Asthenia (HERDA), 74
Hind leg boots, 60, *60*
Hind leg conformation, 77
Hindquarters, softness drills for, 104, *105*
Hock injuries, 73
Hondos. *See* Eyes (hondos)
Hooves, size of, 76
Horn, of saddle. *See* Saddle horns
Horn wraps, *41*, 42, 90
Horsemanship
  balance of activities, 104

ground handling, 98–99, *98–99*
  importance of, 95–96
  mounted roping prerequisites, 97–98
  riding skills, 100–104
Horses. *See also* Exercise and training
  borrowing/leasing, 67–68
  buying considerations, 68–69
  conformation of, 75–79
  health issues, 69–75
  rider suitability, 69, 98
  size of, 76
Hyperkalemic Periodic Paralysis (HYPP),
  73–74

Impressive bloodline, 74
Incentives, 8
Inherited diseases, 73–75
Injury prevention/treatment, 58–60, 73,
  104
Instructors, 67, 91–92, 104
Internet resources. *See* Websites

Jackpot competitions, 18
Judges, 16, *17*, 115
Junior Looper Program, 29, 90–91

Keepers
  for cinches, 54
  for tie-downs, 8, 55, *56*, *57*
Kick, of rope, 8, 37–38

Lameness. *See* Soundness
Lap-and-tap start, 8
Lateral flexion, 8, 63, 102, *103*
Latigos, materials for, 54
Lay (rope stiffness), 8, 32, 35–37, *36*
Leads. *See* Left lead/right lead, balance of
  work on
Learning resources
  competitions, observation of, 128–129
  instructors, 67, 91–92, 104
  live speakers, 93
  other ropers as, 104, 105
  practice events, 107–109
  reading material, 76, 94
  video recordings, 43, 93, 146
  websites, 22, 43, 91, 93, 101, 131
Left lead/right lead, balance of work on,
  73, 140, 142, *142*
Legal catches, 7, 114
Legs
  conformation of, 76–77
  protective equipment, 58–60, *59–60*
Lemond, JoJo, 21

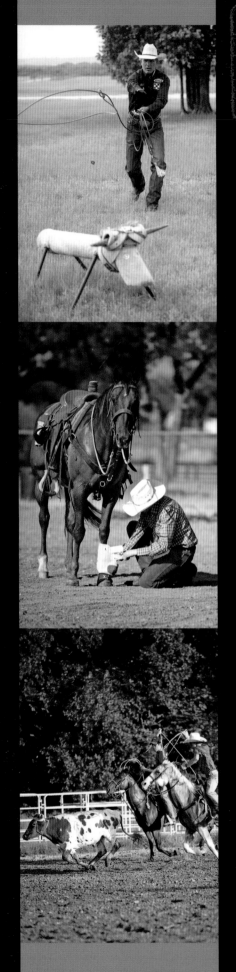

…o Guide
for Getting Started and Getting Good

*Including tips from professional team ropers*
**SPEED WILLIAMS** *and* **RICKEY GREEN**

> The nuts-and-bolts of the sport—what it's all about, including terminology, rules, and regulations.

> The lowdown on ropes, tack, and other equipment.

> What to look for in a horse—from hooves to headset.

> How to handle a rope on the ground, including holding, swinging, and throwing.

> Rider pre-flight checklist—horsemanship skills you can't rope without.

> Simple and essential drills for the roping horse from top trainer Clinton Anderson.

> Working a mechanical steer and catching live cattle—head or heels.

> Putting together the ideal run with a partner and testing your skills against others in competition.

"This book will walk you step by step through picking out the perfect horse to preparing for your first competition; and all the training in between."
—from the Foreword by Clinton Anderson

ISBN 978-1-57076-471-4

9 781570 764714

$24.95 *$27.95 in Canada*
Printed in China

www.horseandriderbooks.com

S0-CMY-026